AFTER LIBERALISATION

After Liberalisation

A Vision of Europe in the Global Economy of the Twenty-First Century

Christopher J. S. Gentle

First published in Great Britain 1996 by
MACMILLAN PRESS LTD
Houndmills, Basingstoke, Hampshire RG21 6XS
and London
Companies and representatives
throughout the world

A catalogue record for this book is available
from the British Library.

ISBN 0–333–60988–3

First published in the United States of America 1996 by
ST. MARTIN'S PRESS, INC.,
Scholarly and Reference Division,
175 Fifth Avenue,
New York, N.Y. 10010

ISBN 0–312–16195–6

Library of Congress Cataloging-in-Publication Data
Gentle, Christopher J. S. , 1966–
After liberalisation : a vision of Europe in the global economy of
the twenty-first century / Christopher J. S. Gentle.
p. cm.
Includes index.
ISBN 0–312–16195–6
1. Europe—Economic integration.   2. Economic forecasting—Europe.
3. Deregulation—Europe.   4. Competition, International.   I. Title.
HC241.G38   1996
337.4—dc20   96–19546
                                                            CIP

© Christopher J. S. Gentle 1996

10   9   8   7   6   5   4   3   2   1
05   04   03   02   01   00   99   98   97   96

Printed and bound in Great Britain by
Antony Rowe Ltd, Chippenham, Wiltshire

For Jackie

Contents

List of Tables and Figures

TABLES

FIGURES

Preface

The inspiration for writing this book came from the dramatic changes that I have seen taking place throughout European business and society in the early 1990s. I have been fortunate enough to work on projects both for the European Commission at CURDS – the academic consultancy at the University of Newcastle upon Tyne – and for a number of Europe's leading corporations, clients of The Henley Centre – Europe's premier business consultancy – enabling me to experience these dynamics of change at first hand. What I have seen over the last five years, in contrast to the euphoria of the late 1980s, has been a Europe characterised by a more sober and realistic vision of the future. At the heart of this realism is how will Europe compete in the global economy of the twenty-first century.

The quest for improved industrial competitiveness has come to dominate the agenda for change in Europe. The rise and rise of an increasingly integrated global economy has intensified this debate. Simply, the core of the argument is: can unfettered market forces alone bring Europe greater prosperity?

Undoubtedly, the introduction of the single European market was a necessary stimulus to modernise what was an increasingly inefficient industrial structure. Throughout the 1970s and early 1980s, European industry moved lethargically with little effort to rise to the challenge of growing international competition. Business had grown fat on the cosy national linkages and partnerships that were protected by government regulatory and procurement policies.

Now is a key point in Europe's development to evaluate and assess these factors. Economic fundamentals are shifting more rapidly than ever before. Europe must now pit its labour force against that of China – which has labour rates that are some 30 times cheaper. Political changes mean that Europe stands at an important junction in its history. The accelerating process of political integration, after the tragic worlds of this century, mean that Europe is now on the brink of an unprecedented unification. Momentum has been added to this unification by the collapse of the Communist bloc and the reunification of Germany.

This book is an attempt to make a valid and significant appraisal of the complex interactions of the factors that will influence the development of Europe over the next generation. The focus is on how these interactions will influence Europe's economic competitiveness, after liberalisation, deregulation and privatisation have taken their course.

The book draws on five years of research and consultancy experience across a range of industries and in the majority of member states of the European Union. Case studies of three business sectors at the leading edge of the market liberalisation, state deregulation and internationalisation bring colour to illustrate the fundamental changes sweeping through Europe. At all times demonstrating the link between forces driving through the global economy and Europe, the book provides an analysis of the implication of liberalisation for economic competitiveness in its widest sense. So it considers not only the prospects for European corporations in their battle against their Japanese and North American rivals, but also the overall prosperity and quality of life for all of Europe's citizens.

Christopher Gentle
London
September 1995.

Acknowledgements

There are many people that I need to thank in the preparation of this book. In the preparation of Chapter 3, I have received help from a number of people. Glen Morgan at Manchester Business School arranged the two conferences in Berlin and Paris that formed the basis of this chapter. Also discussions with Francisco Bosch Font (Cohen & Woolfe, Spain) have been invaluable. Jackie O'Reilly (WZB, Berlin) is always a source of information, ideas and encouragement. Finally, Jean-Pierre Daniel (CREPS, Paris) is always providing interesting topics and ideas for discussion.

For Chapter 4 I must first thank Jeremy Howells, a colleague from my days at CURDS, but now working for the Judge Institute of Management at Cambridge University and the European Commission. He was a major contributor to Chapter 4 on European computer services. Together, we worked closely investigating the implications of a single European market for this industry. Also, I must thank Richard Holway for the information on the European computer services.

A number of people gave me advice and help in writing Chapter 5 on telecommunications. In particular, I would like to acknowledge Andrew Adonis (Financial Times) for his time and ideas. The case study on Spain was made possible by Salvador Segue Cosume (Madrid). Also, I must extend my thanks to senior executives in BT, France Telecom, Siemens, Digital, Andersen Consulting, and Cap-Gemini-Sogeti, which are just a few of the many corporations that have contributed to research on which this book is based.

There are also a number of colleagues and friends I would like to thank. Ewen Peters (Scottish Enterprise) for our chats over a capuccino in Glasgow. Bob Tyrrell (Executive Chairman) and Stephen Radley (Chief Economist) at The Henley Centre for shaping my ideas on globalisation. Fillippo dell Osso (GGT Advertising) has been a constant source of ideas especially on Italy. Feng Li (Napier Business School, Edinburgh) has shared many ideas. Ranald Richardson (CURDS) always gives another view and unconventional opinion. Also, thanks to Jon Guthrie and Caroline White at

The Henley Centre for their assistance in helping with the manuscript.

Finally, this book is for Jackie – my partner. Thanks for your patience, inspiration and editing.

1 Enter the Market, Exit Regulation

EUROPE AT A CROSSROADS

Look around you. What is the Europe of today like? Is it what you expected a decade ago? How is it different? Do you think that Europe is moving towards a closer union? If it is, do you think this movement will be beneficial to your standard of living? Do you want a closer union? Do you think that this process of a move to a closer union will accelerate over the next decade? What factors do you think will shape Europe's future development? What do you think Europe will look like in 2010? These questions are important, because Europe now stands at a crucial junction in its history, largely because of the victory of market forces over regulation.

Europe is at an historic crossroads. The region stands at this junction with a plethora of major forces coalescing which will significantly influence its development over the next 20 years. Europe stands at this crossroads in four ways.

First, Europe stands at a crossroads in its economic development. Key decisions will be taken over the next five years that will have a fundamental bearing on the shape of Europe in the twenty-first century. These decisions will determine the competitiveness of Europe in the world economy. The most important decision to be made surrounds the move to economic and monetary union (EMU). The Maastricht Treaty set Europe on a path to integration, which was supposed to result in the smooth transition to a single currency by the turn of the century. However, the road has been bumpy, progress slow. But as the dawn of the twenty-first century approaches, so too does the immediacy of the decisions to move to closer economic ties. EMU involves far more than just the introduction of a single money for Europe. It requires power to be devolved from nation states into the hands of centralised, and in some instances non-elected, bodies. For example, the Central European Bank (ECB), a non-democratic institution, is to have responsibility for monetary policy. It also

1

means by implication that further political integration must ensue.

Second, Europe is at a crossroads in the way that business and industries are changing. The advent of the single market has brought new market pressures to bear on European business. So great are these pressures that business is reorganising and restructuring to meet this new challenge. The best indicator of the pace of change is merger and acquisition (M&A) activity. For instance, data for the first half of 1995 showed that M&A deals for target companies were worth a record $75.5 billion[1]. Consolidation is taking place in a number of industries. For instance, in all areas of the finance sector particularly insurance, banking and investment banking; in the pharmaceuticals industry; and in telecommunications.

Third, Europe is at a political crossroads. The process of closer economic integration cannot flow without parallel moves to form elected and representative political decision-making bodies. There is a need to ensure that the rapid developments in a single market, followed by the closer economic and monetary union – in whatever shape – is counter-balanced by similar political processes. However, it is not purely economic integration that is bringing change to the political composition of Europe. There is the decline of the nation state on the one hand, and, on the other, the associated rise of regions. Throughout Europe the last decade has seen a drift in power towards the provinces: creating a Europe of the regions. In Germany, Spain, France and Italy regions and cities now have significant political autonomy. The Maastricht Treaty recognised this trend by establishing the Committee of the Regions: a body to oversee the impact of policy emanating out of Brussels on European regions. But the Committee of the Regions is also a non-democratic body. There is also a third dimension to political change. Across the European Union there is a fragmentation of the old post-war political parties. The old system of two large political parties representing left and right wing othodoxies has vanished. It has been replaced by a patchwork of different alliances and allegiances. The traditional system is ravaged by sleaze, scandal and corruption in virtually every country in western Europe. The massive clean-up in Italian politics has been the most extreme example, but similar, if not quite as damaging events have happened in almost every EU country, especially Britain, Belgium, Spain and France.

European society is also at an important crossroads. Since the early 1980s it has been clear that the old post-war structures of a job-for-life and the nuclear family have been eroded. As unemployment has become more common, so too has crime as Europe's once peaceful and safe streets have become more violent. Beneath these trends is the divergent social fragmentation of European society. The family, the glue that held together economic development and society, is being ravaged by pressures from the economic arena. These include the pressures on wage rates brought about by competition from the low-wage economies of the developing world, and the gradual withdrawal of the post-war welfare safety net.

Finally, significant changes are taking place in the international arena, which are redefining the role that Europe must play in this arena. Traditionally, the globe was divided into rich countries with high rates of productivity and high wages, and poor countries with low productivity and low wages. But now, the playing field has changed. A growing number of countries have now fused together high productivity with low wages. At a world level, this has changed the whole economic game. The distinction between developed and developing economies is blurring and, because of this it is causing the redistribution of productive assets across the globe. It is no longer possible for Europe to easily maintain rising standards of living. Again, this force is leaving Europe at a new departure point in its history.

Europe, then, is at a significant crossroads – a once in a century occurrence. But, why have these specific trends come together at the end of the twentieth century? This book is about one of the key forces behind this change – liberalisation. For over the last 20 years the philosophy of the market has gained greater and greater credence. First in the USA under the two Reagan administrations. Then in Europe. In Britain under the three Thatcher governments. Slowly the ethos of the market spread to continental Europe, particularly along the corridors of the European Commission in Brussels. Today, the market is all pervasive in Europe.

WHAT IS LIBERALISATION?

Let us deal first with the question: what is liberalisation? There are many different forms of liberalisation. Indeed, liberalisation has different meanings for many different groups of society. For governments, liberalisation has been adopted as a part of the ideological shift that has occurred over the last two decades. This shift has been denoted by the movement away from big government. The vogue has been for administrations to withdraw from ownership of industries and open up markets to international competition. It has been associated with government crusading against restrictive practices in industry, to reduce inefficiencies, enhance competitiveness, and to mobilise popular political support.

For corporations, liberalisation is associated with the cutting of red tape and bureaucracy. Freeing markets and increasing the level of competition. Liberalisation also results in the entry of foreign corporations into formally protected domestic markets. In turn, this results in corporate acquisitions and mergers, and the restructuring of an industry.

For trade unions, liberalisation is often associated with the freeing up of labour markets. To reduce restrictive practices and to instil greater flexibility in the workforce in the face of the growing threat of cheaper labour in developing economies.

Finally, liberalisation includes the changes that have been negotiated at an international level within the GATT (General Agreement on Tariff and Trade) framework. The talks were started in the aftermath of World War II and have gradually introduced a freer environment for trade. Completed in 1994, these multi-national talks mark a watershed in the history of the world: creating a global shift in patterns of trade. In essence, the agreement reduces barriers to trade between countries, facilitating a freer global market. The ending of these talks has also established a new framework for future global liberalisation: the World Trade Organisation (WTO).

The definition of liberalisation used in this book encompasses as broad a church as possible. It includes the freeing of markets from excessive rules: the European Commission has exerted considerable pressure; both through its single European market initiative and afterwards by proposing directives for opening sectors up to competition not included in the initial 1992 programme. It includes the process of the transfer of industries from the state to the private sector. This entails the hand-in-hand process of privatisation and liberalisation of formerly state-owned industries. Finally, it also includes the removal of barriers to world trade. By adopting this broad definition, it is possible to capture the dramatic shifts in ideology that have characterised the arrival of the free-market economy. The degree of liberalisation and, on the other hand, regulation are the defining features of all types of economic system: characterised by the titanic struggle between different forms of capitalism.

CAPITALISM AGAINST CAPITALISM

The birth of capitalism took place in Europe amongst the fledgling industries of the eighteenth century. It has, however, journeyed a long way since its inception. Capitalism has been adopted around the globe over the last 200 years. The challenge posed by communism during the twentieth century has come and gone. The only major lasting scar on capitalism of its battle with communism, has been its lasting orientation towards the production of arms to fight the cold war. John Kenneth Galbraith[2], believes this development has fundamentally changed the make up of the USA – seen by many as capitalism in its purest form – in that such a large part of government resources are now focused on the production of military hardware.

Although born in Europe, capitalism has flourished most successfully in the USA and Japan. The forms it has taken in these two economies are distinctly different from each other. In the USA, capitalism is characterised by the notion of the sacredness of the individual, both as citizen and shareholder. The idea of society has been subverted by the demands of the economic system. And, as noted above, the economy has become skewed to reflect the paranoia of the potential Soviet threat.

In Japan, a different type of capitalism has evolved. The Japanese model is far less individualistic than in the USA. Although it too is focused on private gain, it is the large

industrial groupings or *keiretsu* that have been the main bene-
ficiaries, rather than individual investors. Corporate managers
are urged to reinvest profits in the productive capacity of the
economy, rather than pay it in dividends to maintain the share
price of the company. The final key difference between USA
and Japanese capitalism is the homogenous nature of Japanese
society compared with the heterogeneity of the USA. In Japan,
the vast majority huddle around a notion that they are all of a
very similar class and status – some 90 per cent describe
themselves as middle-class in post-war Japan. Meanwhile, the
USA is composed of a huge ethnic and class mix. For instance,
by early in the next century cities such as Los Angeles and
Miami will have a greater Spanish than English speaking
population.

Within Europe, however, it is difficult to speak of a definitive
form of European capitalism. Indeed, one of Europe's most
enduring features is its diversity. This holds true in the very
different forms of capitalism that can be found in Europe.
There is a variety of forms of capitalism within the melting pot
of Europe: the family capitalism of Italy; the protectionist, state
interventionist and inflation prone models of France and
Spain; the Anglo-Saxon version in Britain, and the very
successful and distinctive Rhine model based around German
capitalism.

Nonetheless, it is possible to identify commonalities that
define a core model of Eurocapitalism, as Michel Albert[3] calls
it. Its defining features are first dominance of a social realm of
welfare. Europeans cluster around the idea of social justice and
cohesiveness, that has built up in the aftermath of World War
II. This social inclusiveness has become the cornerstone of
European society. This is not to say that Europeans are not
fiercely entrepreneurial. The second feature of Eurocapitalism
is the high propensity for small firms to dominate local
economies. In Germany, Italy, France and Spain small and
medium enterprises are the lifeblood of the economy. The
third feature that differentiates Eurocapitalism is the high
degree of government involvement in the economy – to
achieve social cohesiveness. Government's share of the
economy (gross national product) in most European countries
is between 45 and 55 per cent, by contrast Japan and the USA
are at half that level. Finally, Eurocapitalism is characterised by

cross-ownership of corporations. Financial institutions have large equity stakes of major industrial conglomerates. This cross-ownership model is credited with giving industry a longer term investment horizon than that possible under the shareholder capitalism of the USA and Britain.

As the global economy grows and with the fall of communism, a new world order is emerging. What advantages might the present form of European capitalism give it to succeed in the next century? The key factors of many of the potential advantages of Eurocapitalism are as follows. Europe has a genuine international outlook. In part derived from its colonial history, Europeans have always sought to conquer new markets around the globe. Eurocapitalism gains strength from its diversity. The subtle differences in capitalism across Europe noted above give it a wide range of experience on which to draw, and a broad and mature base for future growth. There is also an essential counterweight to this diversity: social cohesion. Europe's social coherence is a key to its future prosperity.

The future of Europe's economic competitiveness will be determined by the head-to-head battle between Anglo-Saxon capitalism and the existing Eurocapitalism. So far, the major impacts of Anglo-Saxon capitalism on its European cousin are the notion of free and unfettered markets, deregulation and small, non-interventionism government. The rise and rise of the free market ideology was fed into Europe by Britain, through the Thatcher governments of the 1980s. Its influence has become much wider and has been embedded in the thinking of key decision-makers. More to the point, policy-makers were inspired to use its neo-classic liberalising logic as the foundation for building the single European market. In the implementation of the single market programme, it became plain in the early 1990s that there was a direct conflict between these Anglo-Saxon features of capitalism, and the dominant form of capitalism in much of Europe.

At issue then is what influence will Anglo-Saxon capitalism have on Europe's future. What will be the impact of liberalisation? How will it affect European capitalism in the future? At what pace and, in what direction will liberalisation take the European economy? This is the purpose of this book: to determine how Europe will look after liberalisation.

LIBERALISATION AND COMPETITIVENESS

In recent decades the market has gained more credence in the benefits it can bring to economic activity: the market has gained economic credibility. In the past, economic theory advocated that the state was required to play a central role in the functioning of an economy. The role of the state in this theory was three-fold.

First, it had a role to take industries into state ownership for the national good. Such industries included utilities such as gas and water, railways, mail and parcels, and telecommunications. Some countries in Europe went further and brought a whole range of 'strategic' industries into state ownership: think here of cars, airlines and steel. The rationale was to protect both the country and the consumer from international competition and the worst effects of free markets.

Second, the government had an important role to play in directly controlling the market. It achieved this aim by the use of regulation. The rationale behind the use of regulation was to place controls on industries to stabilise markets. Quite correctly, markets were seen as having very poor self-correcting mechanisms. This regulatory action came in the aftermath of the depression of the late 1920s and early 1930s. It was clear from the disastrous effects of the events such as the Wall Street Crash in 1929 that unfettered markets had the power to completely destabilise an economy. In response, governments introduced legislation across a range of industries that would nullify the worst effects of the market. Many governments even went to the extent of encouraging cartels and restrictive practices.

Third, none of this could be achieved without the state taking a controlling interest in the financial system. This involved a detailed segmentation of the financial system, which prevented the side-effects of the malfunctioning of the system from spilling over into other areas of the economy. It also allowed government to have greater macro-economic control, by keeping a close watch over the amount of lending taking place in different sectors of the economy. Hence, in most countries, the central bank was taken into public ownership. For example, in Britain the Bank of England was nationalised in 1947. This gave government control over money, the lifeblood of capitalism.

Today, there has been a fundamental shift in economic theory and practice. The market is now regarded as the most important feature of economic activity. It has the power to harness the wealth generating capacity of an economy. Hence, contemporary economic theory is focused on how best to make the market operate. Central to this philosophy is the reduction in the amount of regulation in an economy: high regulation equates to a sluggish, inefficient economy, while a liberalised open economy is lean and highly efficient. By liberalising large parts of an economy, in particular the barriers that protected it from global competition, countries can gain virtue and kudos in the international community. In short, the degree of liberalisation is now globally associated with improved economic competitiveness.

This book challenges the notion that the degree of liberalisation directly equates to improved economic competitiveness. The market has many strengths. It should be the motor that is used to harness the wealth creating potential of an economy and to raise standards of living. However, without the restraints of regulation its powerful forces are self-destructive.

As noted earlier, Europe stands at an historic crossroads in its future. The battle to prove the importance of liberalisation to future economic competitiveness is a crucial debate in determining which route Europe should take in the future.

Europe has over the last decade introduced a raft of liberalising directives. The evidence on the extent that liberalisation can confer future economic advantage on Europe is so far mixed. For example, in spite of having some of the highest levels of regulation in the world, in terms of trade, Europe – measured in terms of the largest four economies of Germany, France, Italy and Britain – is the largest exporter of goods in the world (Table 1.1). The proportion of exports per head of population is greater in the European Union (EU) big four than in its USA rival: a population of some 200 million in the EU generated twice the value of exports of a population of 243 million in the USA. It also has a number of the countries – Britain, France, Germany and Italy – that top the league for the export of services (see Chapter 2).

Fundamental changes are taking place in the world economy. In 1994, the world saw the largest increase in world

After Liberalisation

Table 1.1   World Trade 1977–93 (per cent of total goods)

	1977	1981	1985	1989	1993
Germany	11.9	10.0	10.7	12.3	10.3
France	6.0	5.5	5.4	5.9	5.9
Britain	5.2	5.3	5.4	5.1	5.0
Italy	4.1	4.0	4.2	4.7	4.6
Big four EU	27.2	24.8	25.7	28.0	25.8
USA	11.6	12.5	11.9	12.4	12.8
Japan	7.6	8.0	9.6	9.2	10.1
Other	53.6	54.7	52.8	50.4	51.3
Total	100	100	100	100	100

Source: OECD (1994)[4]

trade for 20 years. Germany maintained its position in the top three world exporters. Its performance does not appear to have been hindered by excessive regulation. Indeed, European Union trade statistics for 1994 show that those countries with least liberalisation have the largest trade surplus: Germany has the largest surplus of 25.6 billion* Ecu, Italy a 12.7 billion Ecu surplus and France 10.8 billion Ecu. By contrast, Britain – with the most liberalised economy in Europe – recorded a deficit of 20.7 billion Ecu. Overall, the EU has a trade surplus with the rest of the world of 3 billion Ecu – with exports rising by over 10 per cent in this one year.

Add to this position the level of social welfare in Europe. Without a doubt, Europeans enjoy the highest standard of welfare service in the world. Throughout the last 200 years, Europe has progressively built a social dimension into its version of capitalism. In particular, after World War II, the level of welfare provision was raised so as to bind together its shattered economies. This involved creating state pension systems, national health care networks and the provision of public services at a local level. Together these services have enhanced the quality of life in Europe.

---

* Billion = a thousand million

These systems also have their costs. The changing demographic profile of Europeans means that there is a price to pay. It is a heavy one, too. The greatest potential cost in the next century derives from the state pension systems. The ageing of the population means that there will be a drastic reduction in the ratio of the number of working people to those of retirement age. The problem is that the level of saving in the past has been insufficient to meet the bill of today. Europe's pensions systems are being modernised. Nonetheless, the burden of a maturing population – the problem is worst in Germany and best in Britain – together with an increasing level of welfare to a growing minority of long-term jobless, is having the effect of adding to budget deficits. This is one of the greatest problems that European capitalism faces in the next century. It is also preventing progress on moving towards economic and monetary union. However, these heavy costs although affecting the performance of Europe's major economies are not crippling its economic competitiveness.

Conventional economic theory has suggested that high wage economies, such as Germany, will be unable to compete in the emerging global economy of the twenty-first century. The cost of labour, so existing theory goes, makes the European economy uncompetitive. It cannot be denied that there is a lag between the level of exports and international competitiveness of an economy. This is because structural changes have got to work through a country's economic system. This involves the depreciation of fixed capital investments and the reduction in workforces. Nonetheless, in the turbulence that swept through global currency markets in the spring of 1995, the hot money fled towards Europe and, in particular the Deutschmark: an indication that the markets believed that Germany would remain the strongest future economy in Europe, if not the world. Hardly a sign that the German economy is past its best.

As already noted, economic theory is unable to explain why it is that in the face of conventional negative trends, Germany continues to be Europe's most successful exporter. Another conventional wisdom is that the more liberalised an economy, the more competitive it is in the international marketplace. The sweeping away of the barriers that have formally separated an economy from the events in the international economy, is seen by Anglo-Saxon capitalism as a necessary precondition of

a successful economy. In Britain, for instance, it is argued that
the country needs to throw open its doors to the international
marketplace to be successful. In short, it has been argued that
Britain needs to become the Hong Kong of Europe, with little
or no regulation and minimum government. In this way it is
argued, Britain could become a low-wage, low-cost island
within the European Union, thus gaining a march on its
continental neighbours.

However, for Britain or any other European Union country
to adopt such a strategy would be economic suicide. For it is
impossible for European economies to compete on the same
low-cost basis as developing economies such as China and
India. What is required is an economic framework that can tell
us why it is that a number of European countries have a
substantial trade surplus, yet at the same time have high wage
and relatively inflexible economies. The answer lies not only in
the degree of liberalisation and deregulation that has been
introduced, but that there is a premium associated with the
production of quality goods and services. In attempting to
rationalise why these countries are such successful exporters
credit has to be attributed to the value of the fixed assets of an
economy[5]. This means the micro-structure of the economy: the
quality of infrastructure; the standards, types and levels of
education; the network of trade bodies and unions; the
cohesiveness of the buyer–supplier relationships; and the
entrepreneurial zest of Europeans.

A key characteristic of the future global economy will be the
growing influence of large trans-national corporations (TNCs).
Although these corporations will be the major drivers of
change, it will be small firms that will be the lifeblood of
Europe, especially at the local level where agglomerations of
small firms enhance the value added content of local
economies. Michael Porter[6] has put forward such an idea,
stressing the benefits that clusters of industries can confer at a
local level. For instance, the European Commission estimate
that in private sector services, over half of employment is in
firms of under 100 employees in all member states, except
Belgium[7].

Further evidence to suggest that liberalisation does not
immediately confer business competitiveness comes from
labour markets. Since the late 1970s progressive liberalisation

of Europe's labour markets has taken place, in response to the growing challenge of the international economy. Taking a broad view across business cycles, it can be seen that the employment content of growth has been limited as liberalisation has increased – jobless growth has gone hand-in-hand with liberalisation. Again this suggests that a deeper understanding of the impact of free-markets on the European economy is needed, but also what will be the long-term implications in an era after liberalisation. This book investigates what difference liberalisation will make to individual economies, and more broadly the competitiveness of Europe in the world economy of the next century.

Fifty years after the end of World War II, Europe once again is faced by a dilemma of choices. As the challenges of the global economy move over the horizon, Europe must decide to what degree it should embrace liberalisation and shed the rules that have protected its economies, afforded enduring prosperity, and an unprecedented level of welfare benefits since the end of World War II.

Liberalised, unfettered markets offer Europe the opportunity to rid itself of restrictive practices; to be more competitive in the new world economic order. They offer the opportunity to raise standards of living, by giving consumers lower prices at a higher standard of service. Last, by allowing international capital to flow into Europe, this can renew existing, ageing infrastructure and enable a new digital infrastructure – the Infobahn of the next century – to be built.

Equally, by fully embracing the ethos of liberalisation and the free-market economy, Europe risks the prosperity it has built since the war. Opening its economies fully to the forces of the market, without the necessary social structures in place may well send Europe into a spiral of economic and social crisis. In essence, Europe risks tearing the social fabric that has held it together for the last five decades.

Liberalisation of European service industries – the particular focus of this book – is necessary since these industries will be the motor of economic growth in the twenty-first century. Once sacrosanct, services in the 1990s are undergoing major changes. Europe's next wave of restructuring is at hand, which will radically change the economy; services are at the heart of this change. Liberalisation is the harbinger of these deep changes.

Manufacturing industry has already experienced many of the forces that are now emerging over the horizon for service industries. Manufacturing companies internationalised in the 1970s and 1980s, with harsh consequences for Europe as production was moved to cheaper locations in developing economies. This shake-out radically restructured manufacturing, drastically cutting employment, but enhancing productivity in the long term. Does a similar fate await service industries?

Service industries are quite distinct and are in many ways in their infancy compared with manufacturing. The nature of capitalism has resulted in most developed economies having most employment in services – over six in ten employees are in service-related jobs. In Europe, this is partly due to the growth in public sector employment. It has also been due to the shielding of services by regulation.

However, change is at hand. In collaboration with liberalisation, two factors will have a major bearing on the role services play in economic development.

The first force is technology. Fundamental innovations have come to fruition over the last decade. Most powerful has been the fusion of communication and information technologies (ICTs) on a commercial basis. This new fusion has created a new platform, some term it a revolution, in the way information can be collated, stored, processed and, moved around the globe[8]. Since the raw material of services is information, ICTs have spawned a whole new industry – information services. Developments in technology will become increasingly important in the future as the Internet gains in popularity. But, of greater importance to the commercial world is the emergence of digital technologies that build on ICTs; creating a multi-media world. The foundation of this new world is a communications infrastructure that links economies, corporations and individuals.

As Nicholas Negroponte[9] – of MIT MediaLab fame – points out these developments will fundamentally change the way business is done. It is removing the need for an individual to be in the same place as the job they are undertaking. For instance, you can make an airline reservation with Swiss Air by phone to fly from London to Zürich, the operator is sitting in the Indian sub-continent. Whole industries are also restructuring themselves and converging together: media, telecommunications, computing, software, radio, television.

The second major force which, over the next generation, will affect services is their increasing tradability. Developments in liberalisation and technology have laid a path for more trade in services. Currently, most services are locally based and consumed. However, in the future the removal of regulatory barriers will allow corporations to extend activities overseas and internationalise. Technology will allow services to be consumed at a remote location. For instance, market research data and analysis can be packaged on to a compact disk and used anywhere on the globe.

It is with these major developments in mind that service industries were seen as the most appropriate medium through which to view the impact of liberalisation. Service industries are actually mediating the impacts of liberalisation between the actual removal of laws, regulations and restrictive practices and actual economic outcomes. The rationale for choosing the three sectors that follow in Chapters 3, 4 and 5 is to illustrate in more detail these important trends.

Chapter 3 deals with financial services, which are fundamental to any economic system. Hence, the radical regulatory changes that are sweeping through this industry will have a significant impact on Europe in the next century. Directives under the 1992 programme to create a single market have advanced furthest in establishing a unified market for financial services. This has taken place in two ways: through a process of competitive deregulation and the liberalising of capital controls. Indeed, the abolition of controls on foreign exchange to allow the free movement of capital is at the very heart of the single European market. The finance industry is being redefined by information technologies, changing the rules of engagement for financial services companies operating in European markets.

In Chapter 4 the computer services industry is used to illustrate how a sector restructures in the face of the creation of the single European market. It looks at the role of liberalisation in the loss of corporate control and ownership. The selection of computer services also illustrates the way the

information revolution is changing the European economy –
spawning a new information services industry. The reason for
looking at the computer services industry is that it provides an
insight into changes of public procurement practices. In the
past, Europe was dominated by national alliances between state
procurement and national champion providers in the private
sector. The liberalisation of these cosy relationships has had
significant implications both for national economies and
national champions.

Telecommunication services provide perhaps the best complete example of the impact of liberalisation on European
business and society. In Chapter 5, the fundamental forces of
liberalisation, technological change and globalisation, that are
sweeping through economic activity, are captured by the events
in the telecommunications industry. Prior to the introduction
of liberalisation – which will be completed in 1998 – telecommunication services were dominated by national carriers
that were often part of a post and telegraph and telecommunications group. For instance, in Britain the telephony
carrier was part of the GPO (General Post Office).

Liberalisation has caused a shift from public to private
ownership, with much hype about the creation of a new
information superhighway: Infobahn in Eurospeak. However, it
is also proving to be a painful exercise, with hundreds of
thousands of job losses, as former state monopolies are
exposed to the market. After the separation of British Telecom
from the GPO, it reduced employment by over 100 000 for
example. The chapter goes on to look at the way that internationalisation has radically altered the shape of telecommunication services in Europe. It examines the fundamental shift to the new information infrastructure of the
future. Finally, it investigates how the changes caused by
liberalisation will affect the future shape of the industry.

The main thrust of this book is to show that the liberalisation
of markets has more than addressed the balance of the overly
bureaucratic state economies of the post-war period. It argues
that it is also time to acknowledge that markets need
regulation; markets have poor self-correcting mechanisms. In
short, free-markets alone cannot deliver prosperity in the
twenty-first century.

If Europe fully embraces Anglo-Saxon capitalism it also

must welcome the fragmentation of society – creating instability and externalities that have a significant drag on economic performance. As ever, it is impossible to detach economic implications from social (and political) consequences.

If Europe had stuck with its model of creaking nationalised industries and state-run economic model, then its growth rates would have become increasingly sluggish. Its citizens would have experienced a stagnation of prosperity and, perhaps more importantly, a continued decline in the competitiveness of its industries. However, having embraced the free-market, privatising and liberalising vast tracts of industry, it is time to add a cautionary warning: free-markets do not offer a panacea for future prosperity.

As Europe moves ever closer to the dawn of a new century it is important that the best features of Anglo-Saxon and European capitalism are combined and harnessed. This book examines new ways that Europe might achieve this balance.

An era after liberalisation offers a once-in-a-generation opportunity: to harness the efficiency of markets; especially in service and information industries. The window is now at hand to capture the correct blend; a social market economy that will give greater prosperity to each and every European. An economy that has globally competitive service industries. But an economy that also bestows on its citizens quality public services that can form the fabric of Europe in the next century.

However, it can also potentially have huge negative effects for the functioning of European economies. The operation of free-markets without regulation in the future, will reinforce the polarising effects within society that have been suffered by Anglo-Saxon countries during the 1980s and the early 1990s. For instance, in the USA the top one per cent of family groups had annual incomes that averaged $167 000 and controlled 13.5 per cent of all income before taxes; the top 20 per cent accrued some 51.8 per cent of all incomes before tax. By contrast, some 12.8 per cent of the population lived below the official poverty line of $12 974 for a family of four in the late 1980s[10]. The USA is also characterised by endemic crime and social collapse in many areas of society, which Hamish McRae[11] considers as potentially the greatest threat to the position of global leadership that the USA has held over the last 60 to 70 years. It is critical then that we identify the key trends that are guiding Europe into the next century. This book looks at the extent to which liberalisation has taken place so far – at the effects of liberalisation on economic activities. In which direction – free-market or fortress Europe – are these new forces taking the European economy? And, at what pace are they leading it. This book provides a cogent assessment of these trends. It concludes with a vision of Europe in 2010.

Notes

1. *Financial Times* 11 July 1995.
2. J. K. Galbraith (1992) *The Culture of Contentment.* Penguin. London.
3. M. Albert (1993) *Capitalism against capitalism.* Whurr Publishing. London. See also H. Henzler (1992) The new area of Eurocapitalism *Harvard Business Review.* July–August, pp. 57–69.
4. OECD (1994) *OECD Economic Outlook.* Dec. Organisation for Economic Co-ordination and Development. Paris.
5. Paul Krugman, a US economist has developed this idea in several publications. See, for instance, P. Krugman (1994) Does third world growth hurt first world prosperity? *Harvard Business Review.* July–August, pp. 113–121.
6. M. Porter (1990) *The Competitive Advantage Nations.* Macmillan. London.
7. European Commission (1994) *Employment in Europe.* CEC. Brussels.
8. Li Feng (1995) *The Geography of ICTs.* John Wiley. Chichester.
9. N. Negroponte (1995) *Being digital.* Hodder and Stoughton. London.
10. Galbraith, *op. cit.*
11. H. McRae (1994) *The World in 2020.* Harper Collins. London.

2 The Era of Great Liberalisation

INTRODUCTION

Liberalisation of markets within Europe is a reflection of the shift in ideology that has swept across the world over the last two decades – the era of great liberalisation. The process of liberalisation has not been confined solely to changes in Europe – least of all the long and distant corridors of the European Commission (EC). Therefore this chapter is set within a global context, rather than the parochial events of Europe.

A brief glimpse at the history of the world economy shows that the path that led to the latest phase of liberalisation – the completion of GATT (General Agreement on Tariffs and Trade) in Marrakech, Morocco in 1994 – can be traced to the end of World War II. Events in Marrakech are indeed a significant landmark in the development of the global economy. In essence, it marks the transition of the global economy into a new era. This era will be dominated by the further rise of trade not only in manufacturing, but also increasingly in services – the sleeping giant of world economy.

The key message of this chapter is that it has been liberalisation, through harnessing market forces, that has forged change at the global level right down to the level of every European citizen. The chapter falls into three parts: liberalisation and the world economy, the effects of liberalisation on Europe, and the negative impacts of liberalisation. The first part of the chapter reviews the dramatic changes that have taken place in the world economy, and the fundamental role liberalisation has played in this process. The formation of a unified economy in Europe needs to be viewed in the context of the development of the internationalisation of the world economy – the two are inseparable. A fundamental driving force of the design of the European single market has been the growth of the global economy – the second part of this chapter looks at the cause and effect of this relationship. Notable in

19

these developments has been the liberalisation of service industries in Europe, so that it might maintain a competitive advantage in industries that have both a high-value-added component and which are becoming increasingly tradable.

However, although Europe is in the midst of the wholesale introduction of market forces, liberalisation has also had side-effects. The final part of this chapter looks at the growing polarisation between rich and poor around the globe, a trend which is also becoming increasingly evident within Europe. The widening division across Europe may put at risk the living standards that rapid liberalisation was meant to accelerate. But let us begin this story with the history of the world economy over the last 50 years.

FROM MONOPOLY TO LIBERALISATION: THE ROAD TO FREE MARKETS AND TRADE

The significant changes that are taking place in the structure of world trade have been welling up since the 1930s. The depression at this time ravaged most of the major economies and led to the reconstruction of the world economy after World War II. The foundation for this new era was the solid base of national regulation.

During this reconstruction, state regulation and intervention in the functioning of economies was at its apex: characterised by a high level of nationalisation of industries such as water and energy utilities, airline, telecommunications, and postal services. In addition, the state played a key role in the management of the economy. The triumph of Keynesian economics at that time meant that western industrial economies were based on the principles of government being responsible for demand management, and stimulating the economy through state spending in times of recession. During this period public services experienced their most halcyon days as the health service, education and local government expanded rapidly.

This domestic system dovetailed with international structures that were created with the aim of reconstructing the world economy – that lay in tatters after the ravages of six years of war. These institutions were established at the meeting between the allies at Bretton Woods (USA) in 1944. The big two institutions formed at Bretton Woods were the World Bank and the International Monetary Fund. These two institutions, together with the Marshall Plan – which provided money for the reconstruction of European economies – brought stability and prosperity to the West: the 'we've never had it so good' era to quote Harold Macmillan, a British Prime Minister in the late 1950s.

No longer had this system reached its apogee in the 1960s and early 1970s than the forces that were to radically alter its economic foundations were beginning to assert a degree of influence. These forces of change had been gathering within the international financial and economic systems for some years before the oil shocks of the early 1970s finally unleashed the tidal wave of pressure. Following these events there was break down of the old Keynesian system towards a new market orientated system driven by four inter-related and highly complex trends: globalisation of the world economy; the growth and increasing influence of trans-national corporations (TNCs); new developments in technology; and internationalisation of financial markets.

The liberalisation process in Europe early in the 1980s was a response to these forces, but also to the managed liberalisation of trade within the General Agreement on Tariffs and Trade (GATT). At the broadest level, it was an attempt to maintain the competitiveness of European industry. It is in this context that the liberalisation process must be viewed.

GATT AND THE HISTORIC RESHAPING OF THE WORLD ECONOMY

No single event has had such a profound and far-reaching impact on the world economy as the conclusion of the international trade liberalisation talks, known as GATT. For nearly 50 years now the world economy has been increasingly reshaped by the managed process of the liberalisation process within the GATT framework.

Protectionism in the 1920s and 1930s that caused the depression spurred the international community to build a more managed, but also liberal, international trading system. At first, the structure of national regulations together with restrictive trade practices carried over from the protectionism era, meant that there were still many barriers to economic activity. However, these have been gradually eradicated, so that the average tariff on goods has fallen from 40 per cent at the end of the 1940s to three per cent by the mid 1990s.

A GUIDE TO GATT

In April 1994, the Uruguay Round of GATT was signed by 116 countries in the North African city of Marrakech. By contrast, only 23 countries took place in the original talks held in Geneva in 1947, which were completed within a year. The eighth and final GATT deal took nearly eight years to negotiate. On its completion, GATT was replaced by a new organisation – the World Trade Organisation (WTO). This marks a new start in the liberalisation process, with the focus moving to services, rather than manufacturing; reflecting the shift in economic activity across the globe. The GATT talks had to work very hard to get services included in the negotiations. Indeed, telecommunications and banking were left out of the final agreement, although there have been EU directives to liberalise these two industries.

A single principle bound GATT together: that discrimination prevents trade. All the member countries of GATT embraced the notion that a member opens its market equally to every other country participating in GATT. This had four main benefits. First, it allowed small countries access to bigger countries' markets, that would have been impossible to negotiate outside the GATT framework. The second key benefit was that potential protectionist tendencies, that may have sprouted from soured bilateral trade agreements, were dealt with within GATT. Third, regional trading blocs were only permitted if they included most forms of trade and did not erect barriers to those outside that trading bloc. Finally, GATT allowed for developing economies to be favoured – acting as a lever to gradually open them up to the world economy.

Indeed, the eight rounds within GATT's history have had a profound effect on the world economy. It is estimated that in the 25 years between 1950 and 1975 the volume of world trade expanded five-fold, at the same time as the world economy doubled in size[1].

However, the initiation of the Uruguay Round came about due to growing pains within the world economy. Two factors were particularly important. First, during the 1970s, there were growing tensions within the world economy precipitated by the oil crisis. The USA became very disgruntled about its competitive position as the dollar strengthened within a stagnating world economy. It raised the spectre of protectionism to stimulate new liberalisation initiatives through GATT. The other major force – caused by the rapid advances in technology – was the mushrooming importance of services: changing the very basis of economic activity and patterns of trade.

It is within this context that the talks of the final round of GATT negotiations were initiated. The deal struck at the end of these talks will have profound implications for the world economy over the next decade. It is estimated by GATT that over $200 billion will be added to global gross domestic product (GDP). However, as Table 2.1 shows, these gains will not be evenly distributed across the world; there will be winners and losers. The biggest winner will be Europe which is estimated to gain over $90 billion by early in the next century. By contrast, the developing world is a definite loser, for instance Africa will be worse off after this greatest of all trade deals.

Table 2.1   Gains from GATT. Annual gains from trade liberalisation by 2002 (1992 prices, $ billion)

Asia	62.2
Africa	–2.6
Gulf & Mediterranean	1.5
Latin America	8.0
North America	21.3
Japan	25.9
Former Soviet block	2.1
EU	93.5
World Economy	211.9

Source: *The Economist* 'GATT' 4 December 1993

THE GLOBAL ECONOMY: EXIT THE OLD, ENTER THE NEW

The major force that has driven liberalisation in Europe has come from the growing competitive threat from the world economy. Over the last 30 years there has been a growing dynamism within the world economy. As economic activity has become more international, so too has the rate at which changes have taken place.

Three features have characterised this development. First, the triumph of market capitalism over communism. The dramatic end of the cold war at the close of the 1980s, marked by the collapse of the Berlin Wall, has radically changed the geo-political map of the world. Today, with the exception of North Korea, virtually every country in the world has some form of market economy. This has been a rapid structural change from the position that existed for most of the post-war era when the two Super-Powers – USA and Soviet Union – battled it out to control large parts of the developing world.

Second, there has been the trend to form regional trading blocs. The opening of the world economy has demanded that economies of scale are the most important competitive platform on which to compete. As a result, countries have banded together into regional trading blocs. It has been this logic that has resulted in the formation – over the last decade – of the triad of trading blocs: ASEAN (Association of South East Asian Nations, the trade bloc of the so-called Asian Tigers); NAFTA (North American Free Trade Association); and the SEM (Single European Market). Trade bloc fever has now spread to all parts of the world. For instance, in South America there has been the formation of MERCOSUR: a free-trade area based around Argentina, Brazil, Paraguay and Uruguay. Indeed, it is now proposed that NAFTA and MERCOSUR be merged in 2005 to cover the whole of the Americas – creating the largest free trade area in the world.

The reality of a truly global economy is illustrated by the car industry. According to calculations by the American Automobile Manufacturers, world motor vehicle production in 1993 was almost equally divided between Asia, Europe and North America. This example reinforces the point that in key industries, a global economy is now in operation.

The changes that are taking place in the world economy are monumental. Indeed, it is difficult to get a proper grasp of the size and impact of the flows of goods and capital that now circumnavigate the world. The fundamental shift that has taken place is illustrated by the changing distribution of manufacturing and services across the globe. In 1961, France had 27 per cent of its workforce in manufacturing, compared with South Korea which had just 5 per cent. Compare the same countries in 1991. France has just one in five workers in manufacturing, whereas South Korea has one in four of its workforce[2]. By contrast, developed economies now dominate world markets for services. Taking the example of commercial services – these include professional, business and consulting services, but exclude financial services – the top five exporters of such services in 1992 were: USA, France, Italy, Germany and Britain[3].

The inter-connections within the world economy grow ever more complex. Globalisation can be credited for the growing complexity of economic activity: it is increasingly determining the winners and losers in the world economy at all levels – trade blocs, regions, sectors, companies and even individuals.

Globalisation can be defined as the internationalisation of markets, corporations, production and technology into a seamless world economic system. There are four factors that are underpinning the rise of an integrated global economy: the introduction of liberalisation; the growing influence of transnational corporations (TNCs); the fusion of information and communication technologies; and the internationalisation of financial markets.

First, and foremost, is liberalisation of economic activity – the key concern of this book. The removal of the fetters from all areas of economic activity, from trade, cartels, and market controls through to labour markets, has been inseparable from the growth in the trade of goods, investment and services on an international scale. This close connection between the internationalisation of economic activity and liberalisation – regulation can be traced back through the history of capitalism. The inter-relation between regulation and markets' dynamic has not only created tensions since the inception of capitalism; but is also the very essence of capitalism. At a very broad level economic systems constantly move between states of (stringent) regulation – via liberalisation – to freer markets. And – via re-regulation – in the opposite direction.

Moving hand-in-hand with liberalisation has been the opening up of developing economies. The unleashing of the market economy on developing economies has been channelled via two principal routes. First, through multi-national governmental organisations, in particular the World Bank. This organisation has adopted pro-market economic policies which incentivised developing economies into introducing market mechanisms, in return for financial assistance and privatisation expertise. Second, much of this expertise has come through consultancies that first devised the implementation procedures in the USA and Britain. The shift in the global political climate from Keynesian- to market economy-led has resulted in the growth of a number of economies in Latin America and South East Asia. Most notable has been the explosive – if unsustainable double digit – growth of China in the early 1990s.

The second key factor that has brought about an integrated global economy has been the growth of TNCs. As already mentioned above, the car industry now operates on a worldwide basis. However it is only because car companies, such as Ford and General Motors from North America, Volkswagen from Europe, and Toyota and Nissan from Japan, took up the global challenge by building cars in markets outside their traditional stronghold, that the world economy did internationalise. This international behaviour of large corporations is – in the words of Kenichi Ohmae[4] – creating a borderless world:

> *Before national identity, before local affiliation, before German ego or Italian ego or Japanese ego – before any of this comes the commitment to a single, unified global mission. You don't think any longer that the company you work for is a Japanese automaker trying to build and sell its products in the USA. You work for Honda or Nissan or Toyota. The customers you care about are the people who love your products everywhere in the world . . . Country of origin does not matter. Location of headquarters does not matter. The products for which you are responsible and the company that you serve have become denationalised.*

The third factor has been the fusion of information and communications technologies. The coming together of these technologies has shrunk geography for many corporations, enabling them to operate on an international scale more efficiently and effectively. This has happened in two ways. First, it has allowed TNCs to manage a global business from a handful of powerful strategic hubs. For instance, from a global product HQ in Geneva, Switzerland, it is possible to manage the activities, on a minute-by-minute basis, of production in all that company's Latin American production facilities. Second, technology has allowed companies to remotely enter or service distant markets. Perhaps the best example of the use of technology in this way is in financial services.

The final development that has facilitated globalisation has been the internationalisation of capital. The revolution that swept through the world's financial markets has been well documented. Adrian Hamilton[5] described it as a 'revolution in the way finance was organised, a revolution in the structure of banks and financial institutions and a revolution in the speed and manner in which money flows around the world'.

The importance of these changes in the financial structure of the world economy cannot be stressed too greatly – indeed, they play a fundamental part in the story of the liberalisation of Europe. Further, the expansion and integration of capital markets of an international basis allowed the world's largest corporations to more easily finance and manage the risk on their investment plans. Perhaps more significantly, it also facilitated the shift in funding major corporate powerplays from equity to debt based finance. Newly formed international capital markets were more suitable for providing liquidity and spreading risk.

Of the four factors that have combined to produce the globalisation of the world economy, it has been the role of TNCs that has been most significant. The growing power and influence of TNCs is manifesting itself in two key ways: large TNCs are becoming increasingly dominant in market power; and the techno-organisational revolution that is sweeping through businesses of all sizes has increased the power of TNCs.

THE RISE AND RISE OF TRANS-NATIONAL CORPORATIONS

The rise and rise of TNCs has been dramatic over the last few decades. The importance of large firms is illustrated by the growth in turnover of the largest 200 TNCs compared with economic growth rates in the world's major economies. Using data from the European Commission and the OECD between 1986 and 1990, the turnover of the world's largest corporations has outstripped economic growth in Europe, Japan and the USA.

In 1986, the turnover of the largest 200 corporations increased by 3.1 per cent compared with 2.9 per cent, 2.6 per cent and 2.7 per cent in Europe, Japan and the USA respectively. By 1990 the gap had grown significantly wider: turnover grew by over 7 per cent for the largest TNCs against 3 per cent, 5.6 per cent and 0.9 per cent for each of the major economic areas. Indeed, many of the world's largest corporations are now economically more powerful than sovereign states. For instance in the fiscal year to June 1994 Toyota – a Japanese-owned car manufacturer – had net sales of over $94 billion, while in the same fiscal year Du Pont – a US chemicals and plastics producer – sales totalled nearly $37 billion. By contrast, in 1993 Ireland had a GDP of just $23 billion.

In addition to this rising economic power, TNCs are increasingly driving economic change. One way this is taking place is through the growing influence of corporate brands. The visual image of a CocaCola icon, a McDonalds logo or a Volkswagen badge now communicates not just a mere consumer product – but the whole ethos of consumer capitalism. The advent of a global media industry fuelled by major Hollywood blockbusters is just one of the means by which these powerful images are flashed around the world.

More important, however, has been the techno-organisational revolution (TOR) that has transformed TNCs. The TOR has been a key factor in enabling TNCs to achieve growth rates quicker than the largest economies, in particular allowing them to operate more efficiently and effectively. Essentially, as shown in Table 2.2, this revolution is radically restructuring and reorganising five areas at the heart of any

Table 2.2   How the 'techno-organisational revolution' is changing business

Organisation	Breaking down old corporate barriers; facilitating geographical relocation and the separation of activities.
Operations	Shrinking product cycles reduce deficits, and cut bureaucracy.
Staffing	Delayering corporate hierarchies, cutting employment.
New Products	Feedback loops: enhanced marketing effectiveness.
Buyer–Supplier Links	Exploitation of economies of scale; placing demands on suppliers.

Source: The Henley Centre

large corporation. The role of new information and communication technologies in this process has been fundamental. The so-called networking of the corporation has enabled many of these changes to be implemented and managed.

In the context of facilitating the rise of the global economy it has been the changes in the organisational structures of TNCs that have been most crucial. The networking of the corporation has allowed old corporate barriers to be broken down. The separation of conception and design from production has ensued. The opening-up of developing economies has provided cheap labour for the production of goods formerly made in the industrial heartlands of Europe and the USA.

However, it is wrong to assume that this is a trend that is purely affecting manufacturing. Far from it. There is a growing cohort of companies in a range of service industries that are now exploiting the differentials that exist around the world with increasingly sophisticated telecommunications networks. For instance, Bangalore, India (or Electronic City as it is known) has become a popular centre with TNCs, such as IBM,

Hewlett Packard and Sanyo, for software production. The labour intensive process of machine code writing (the basis for software operating systems) takes place in vast software factories staffed by well-educated, but low paid (by western standards) Indians.

A NEW WORLD ECONOMIC ORDER

The consequences of globalisation are, without doubt, profound – creating a new world economic order. There are three features that mark the transition to this new world order. First, a shifting economic powerbase of the world economy – for Europeans – from west to east. Second, the prospects for Europe are increasingly being determined by global trends, in wages, innovative capacity, and business competitiveness. Finally, this all adds up to a painful transition for old, globally non-competitive industries and economies. As the world economy has become increasingly integrated, Europe's economies have been prised open to a new world of commercial pressures and demands.

First, the most prominent feature of this new world economic order is the shifting economic powerbase. Basically, there has been an eastwards shift away from North America and Europe to the Far East, so that South East Asia leads the world in economic growth rates. McRae[6] has distilled five factors from Asian economies that have underpinned this shift:

1. Industrial flexibility, with great ability to move from the manufacture of one product to another.
2. Rapid product imitation or development.
3. A high savings ratio.
4. A culture orientated towards educational achievements.
5. Societies instilled with a work ethic.

This potential has been recognised by international investors, and this is illustrated by the shifting tides of foreign direct investment around the world over the last decade. The introduction of TOR reforms to the structure of major TNCs has allowed an atomisation of costs within the companies. For instance, placing labour intensive operations into low wage

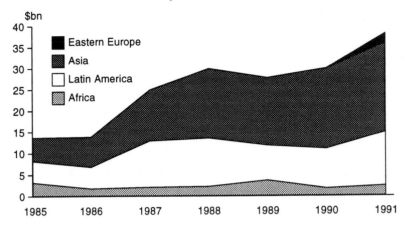

Figure 2.1   Shifting sands: flows of foreign direct investment into developing countries

Source: *The Economist* 'World Economy Survey' 30 September 1993. The Henley Centre 1994

economies. A measure of these changes is shown in Figure 2.1 by the ebb and flow of foreign direct investment.

This United Nations data shows the dramatic shift that has taken place even over the last five years from the old industrial world to the new economic powerbase. In 1990, inflows of foreign direct investment were $175 billion into industrialised economies compared to just $30 billion into developing economies. By 1993 this gap had narrowed to just $30 billion, with investment into developed economies falling by about 40 per cent: $110 billion against $80 billion into developing economies. A gauge of the shift to the Far East is illustrated by the flows of investment into China. Between 1988 and 1992, it is estimated that some $25 billion were invested in China.

Second, the growing integration of the world economy has meant that the differentials between economies have become increasingly magnified and exploited. Perhaps the most visible representation of this trend has been the difference in wage levels between the developed and developing economies. The gap that exists between the highest wage locations and those at the bottom of the league are great indeed.

Factory wages in 1993 range from $25 per hour in western Germany to below a dollar in China – Germany is still, however, the world's largest exporter of manufactured goods[7]. There is also a stratification taking place in the west: Japan, USA and France having wage rates in manufacturing over $15, while others – notably Britain and Spain – have hourly earnings of a little over $10. However, developing economies nearly all exhibit wage structures with manufacturing wages below $5 per hour, with the vast majority below $2.50 – witness Mexico at $2.40, Poland at $2.00 and, as mentioned above, China at around 70 cents per hour.

The final trend in the world economy has been the shifting sectoral composition of the world economy. The exploitation of the differentials in wages has been translated into high wage industries relocating to low wage economies. But this has simply not been a shift in manufacturing to developing economies; it has been characterised by the separation of functions within companies. So that although the general movement of the last two decades has been the exporting of manufacturing production from west to east, there has been a more complex movement whereby – manufacturing or services – labour intensive activities are relocated in low wage economies. For instance, this might involve a manufacturing company where design, marketing and management of a product are undertaken in a developed economy, while production and assembly take place in the developing world.

The sectoral implications of this emerging divide are reflected by the distribution of Foreign Direct Investment (FDI) between 1975 and 1990. Data from the United Nations shows that over this period investment into developed economies in manufacturing industries has fallen from 56 per cent to 42.5 per cent, while an increase from 31.4 per cent to 48.4 per cent has taken place in services. The picture emanating from developing economies is more complex. Although the actual balance of FDI between manufacturing and services has remained relatively stable – roughly 50 per cent in manufacturing and a quarter into both services and primary sectors – in absolute amounts, there has been a huge increase in manufacturing into developing economies: from $19 billion to $102 billion between 1975 and 1990.

These trends are merely a reflection of a more fundamental shift within the economic system. Radical changes are sweeping through the international economy and TNCs; most notably resulting in the separation of design and marketing from the production and assembly. The significance of this shift cannot be stressed too highly. For it provides the basis for which the international economy is founded; knowledge intensive activities in developed economies versus labour intensive processes in developing economies. It is within this context that services will internationalise.

THE DEVELOPING GLOBAL SERVICE ECONOMY

Over recent decades, the global economy has largely grown due to the internationalisation of manufacturing activity. Supporting this expansion has been a range of perfunctory services such as banking and accountancy. This model dominated until GATT began to liberalise services. As a result, the internationalisation of services has made them an important driving force in their own right and the most significant component of growth in the world economy. The international awakening of service industries will be a key force of the global economy of the next century.

Over the last three decades dramatic shifts have taken place in the contribution of services to economic growth. In developed market economies World Bank[8] figures show that the contribution of services to gross domestic product has increased from 54 per cent to 61 per cent between 1965 and 1987. By comparison manufacturing has seen a five per cent decline from 40 per cent to 35 per cent over the same time period. Developing economies are also seeing a growth in the complexity of economic activity. Services have increased their contribution to the GDP of developing economies by around two per cent from 40 per cent to 42 per cent over the same time frame. However, it has been manufacturing that has been the main engine of growth – developing economies experienced a seven per cent increase from 31 per cent to 38 per cent over the 22 years between 1965 and 1987.

Prior to the breakdown of the post-war economic system, services were closely guarded by government regulation. Regulation was enacted to protect the local orientation of services. Think, for instance, of postal services, banking and telecommunication services as suitable examples. Tight government regulation also sealed such services off from competition – creating monopolies such as national rail services.

The rationale used by Government for regulating service industries was based around two key promises. First, a cultural ideology based around the political consensus built up in the aftermath of World War II. For example, in Britain the incoming Labour government established a country-wide health system – the National Health Service – within a wider welfare safety system. In addition, there are other state monopolies that are culturally unique and which give countries their distinctive characteristics: the monopoly that the Italian government has over the sale of tobacco and salt – Sali e Tabacchi – is a classic example. The second basis for national regulation was strategic. Governments decided that particular industries were and would continue to be of strategic importance to economic development. Within the pluralist politics of the 1950s and 1960s industries, such as telecommunications and banking, were taken into state ownership.

As economic development has continued apace and increased in complexity, services and manufacturing have become more inter-dependent and inter-linked. This is a result of the growing complexity of economic activity which has fostered the boom in services. In the bulging nexus of the world economy services have played a key role. Moving beyond the traditional model whereby services followed and supported manufacturing industries, services now lubricate the means of production, distribution and exchange. The dividing line between production and additional tertiary activities has been blurred for good. In today's global economy – facilitated by information technology – services play the fundamental role in the generation of wealth: services make the world go round[9].

If we look in more detail, services can internationalise in two ways: migration and trading. Migration of services to local markets can take place in a number of ways, through direct investment, licensing a franchise, the establishing of joint venture companies or sub-contracting arrangements. All these offer options to enable a service company to construct a bridgehead in a new market. Indeed, this method of establishment has always been available. It is the second option, tradable services, that has radically altered the shape of the world economy. In the past it has been difficult to trade services since many services need to be consumed in the local market.

The branching of sophisticated telecoms networks is rapidly changing this situation. Since many service activities can be dealt with over the wire – whether it's a video-conference with a management consultant or a hotel reservation centre – this has allowed services to be detached from the local market. The use of toll-free numbers, private corporate networks or the world-wide web of the Internet will continue to foster this trend.

These developments need to be viewed in the context of the increasing inter-dependence and inter-linkages between goods and services. It is this relationship that is key to the integration of the global economy. For example, the export and sale of personal computers requires a service guarantee. A consumer is unlikely to invest a significant sum into a 'big ticket', complex consumer good without a local service back-up. The exponential boom Europe-wide in sales' volumes of personal computers poses a problem for the manufacturer in servicing potential customers from Stockholm to Palermo, Dublin to Vienna. The solution for many TNCs is a toll-free or low-cost telephone helpline. The helpline number is a local toll-free or low-cost call, which unknown to the caller can be routed to an international call-centre. Call line identification technology allows the operator in the call centre to know which country the call originated from and to prepare the correct greeting: be it 'Good Morning'; 'Hola'; or 'Pronto'. Hewlett Packard, the US computer manufacturer, operates such a set-up with a call-centre in Holland staffed by 200 personnel.

Clearly, TNCs play a key role in forging new patterns of economic development. For TNCs the difference between goods and services is of diminishing importance. Basically, TNCs look for two market features in the key economic regions of the global economy: the ability to gain market presence, and the ability to compete free from regulations which might place them at a disadvantage against domestic suppliers. In terms of trade the only thing that is vital is the flow of information from the market: the lifeblood of any economic activity. In this sense, telecommunications enable TNCs to fine-tune the types of products and services to what the market demands.

Two major messages are distilled from this analysis. First, that the role of information and communication technologies is becoming increasingly fundamental to the operation not only of individual TNCs, but also for the functioning and growth of the global economy. Second and most important, is that the extent of government regulation and the degree of liberalisation is a key to the openness and competitiveness of a market. The influence of government has been to create a self-fulfilling liberalisation–globalisation cycle. A cycle in which the forces of globalisation are a further pressure for liberalisation. In turn, liberalisation is a necessary process to facilitate further globalisation.

LIBERALISATION, PRIVATISATION AND THE SINGLE EUROPEAN MARKET

In the aftermath of World War II, Europe's shattered economies were bound together to seek greater security and economic prosperity in closer economic integration. In 1956, the Treaty of Rome set down the ground rules for the integration of Europe's leading economies. Throughout the following three decades, closer economic and political integration ensued with a number of other countries joining the original six members: Belgium, Denmark, France, Germany, Italy and the Netherlands. During this period, growing volatility within the world economy, owing to internationalisation of production of trade, was in part responsible for the members of the EU following a closer path to economic, monetary and political union.

Four core principles underlie economic unification in Europe: the liberalisation of goods, capital, labour and services is the basis for economic integration in Europe. The key to the completion of the single market was the adoption of the principle of mutual recognition of national regulations in preference to complete harmonisation. This was because many Member States saw other national regulations either as inadequate protection for consumers or as non-tariff barrier to trade and investment. Integration is to be extended to full Economic and Monetary Union (EMU) by the Maastricht Treaty signed in 1991, but the proposed timetable has been somewhat derailed.

Meanwhile, economic integration continued apace as TNCs

sought to reorganise their business activities on a pan-European basis. In 1985, the then European Community drafted a White Paper in an attempt to keep pace with this process through legislative integration. As it is now well known, the Single European Act – which came into force in July 1987 – aimed to create a unified internal market via the harmonisation of physical, technical and fiscal barriers in nearly 300 areas of business by 1 January 1993. This was largely achieved, although the actual implementation still varies quite markedly between countries.

The basis for operating in a single market is the idea of a single passport, whereby companies are regulated in their home countries, rather than in the host country. This system has created a process of competitive deregulation, where each country in the EU reduces its domestic regulation to be comparable with the country of the least resistance. The crucial point to note is that now that TNCs are in the ascendancy in the global economy, each regional trading bloc must compete in a process of competitive liberalisation so as to attract TNCs and remain competitive.

With the birth of the single market, the process of reorganising the corporate geography of the new Europe was officially initiated. This process, however, is not new. It has been underway for several years, if not decades. Indeed, before the completion of the single market, 40 per cent of all merger and acquisition activity in the EU took place across national borders[10]. Economic history also tells us that since the establishment of overseas production plants by US companies in Britain at the turn of the century – the first being the Singer factory on the River Clyde, Glasgow (Scotland) – TNCs have been entering European markets.

It is within this historical context that the liberalisation in Europe needs to be viewed. The agenda for the creation of a single market was largely driven by the desire to gain economic strength to compete in the more competitive global economy – as outlined above. This pressure coerced Europe to take its economic integration process further – via liberalisation. It was this economic imperative that forced the liberalisation of the European economy.

HAND-IN-HAND: LIBERALISATION AND PRIVATISATION IN EUROPE

Liberalisation has been the main instrument used to introduce market forces into Europe. Europe, however, is characterised by the high level of state control. Liberalisation alone has not proved sufficient to install free-markets. To achieve this aim, liberalisation has been closely entwined with privatisation: in most instances moving hand-in-hand. While privatisation enhances the productive efficiency, the allocation of goods and services in the market; liberalisation reduces monopolies, improves the competitive environment and devolves ownership to share-holders.

Across the EU the public sector has widely different shares of GDP: over 21 per cent in Portugal, to only four per cent in Britain (Table 2.3). These wide differences reflect the level of state involvement in the economy – in essence, the degree to which each post-war government felt it necessary to take various portions of the economy under its wing, within the context of the development of Bretton Woods, the Marshall Plan and GATT.

This level of state-ownership began to be reversed in Europe in the early 1980s. Following the lead of the USA in breaking the AT&T telecommunications monopoly, the Thatcher government in Britain pioneered the privatisation of large parts of state industry. This trend has been adopted beyond Europe and the West, so that virtually every country has undertaken the sale of state property. The World Bank estimates that around 15 000 firms have been privatised since 1990[11].

Privatisation programmes, which have gradually spread to France, Germany and Italy, are radically altering the structure and ownership of these economies. For instance, the privatisation schemes in France and Italy – since 1992 to 1996 – are likely to bring the public sector shares of the two economies down by around 5 per cent to 10 and 15 per cent respectively.

Vast areas of European industry are now ear-marked for privatisation. Governments have been cajoled by a raft of EU directives in a range of industries into selecting their prime industries to sell off to international investors. From the Baltic to the Mediterranean, the governments of the EU have

Table 2.3   Public sector in EU economies (all figures 1991)

	% GDP	% workforce	of which industry	of which fin. services
France	15.1	13.4	3.5	1.5
W. Germany	10.0	8.3	0.6	1.4
Italy	20.0	13.5	2.8	2.3
Britain	4.0	4.3	0.0	0.1
Spain	8.0	6.0	1.2	0.3
Portugal	21.5	10.6	2.0	2.4
Belgium	7.5	9.8	0.2	1.2
Holland	8.0	5.1	0.0	0.0
Greece	17.0	14.7	0.5	3.3
Denmark	8.7	8.2	0.2	0.0
Ireland	11.5	8.7	0.4	0.5
Luxembourg	5.2	3.2	0.0	1.3
EU 12	10.9	8.9	1.3	1.1

Source: Banque Paribas (1995)

privatisations underway with a price tag of $100 billion in 1995[12].

In summary, liberalisation in Europe has taken place with the introduction of the single market and the privatisation of state firms. Liberalisation has not, therefore, left untouched any part of private and public industry.

A CASE STUDY: THE EUROPEAN INSURANCE INDUSTRY

A microcosm of these changes, as part of liberalisation of national markets, is the insurance industry. In 1994, all Member States had to implement new rules that allowed insurers registered in any state to trade throughout the EU. Consequently, national controls over the types and price of general insurance – that is all insurance concerned with insuring property, motor, travel and non-human risks – had to be amended.

Early attempts at creating pan-European companies, in the late 1980s dash for a unified Europe, resulted in many over-priced acquisitions. The Europe-wide recession of the early 1990s placed a drag on activity. Nonetheless, it is now possible to distinguish a European market. Recent years have seen a growing number of such purchases. For instance, in 1994 Switzerland's Winterthur bought one of Germany's largest insurers, DBV. Sun Alliance became the largest insurer in Denmark when it purchased local company Hafnia. Finally, Commercial Union bought Groupe Victoire, France's sixth largest insurance company, in 1994. Corporate giants from Germany, France, Italy and Britain now command a sub-stantial and growing proportion of premium income (Table 2.4).

Another essential feature of the liberalisation of the European insurance market is that companies are using alternative methods of market entry. Most notable is entry through new distribution strategies – using direct selling via the telephone. Thus a company can serve a number of national markets from a centralised telephone operation from one (often low-cost) location – as in the case of the PC market. This

Table 2.4   Europe's top ten insurers (premium income Ecu bn 1993)

		Ecu billion
Allianz	Germany	26.6
UAP	France	19.0
Swiss Re	Switzerland	11.7
Zurich	Switzerland	11.6
AXA	France	11.4
BAT[1]	Britain	10.4
Munich Re	Germany	10.2
Generali	Italy	10.1
Prudential	Britain	9.8
Winterthur	Switzerland	9.3
Commercial Union	Britain	8.7
AGF	France	7.6

[1]BAT includes premium income from US subsidiary Framers Exchanges.

Source: *Financial Times* 13 June 1994

development is fundamentally changing the operation of markets across Europe; breaking the local link with the delivery services.

This example of the insurance industry captures the radical changes that are now sweeping through services in Europe. The combination of new rules, governing the activities of all companies in Europe, and advances in new technologies is reshaping employment patterns, companies and markets in service industries.

THE UNACCEPTABLE CONSEQUENCES OF LIBERALISATION

The final part of this chapter demonstrates that liberalisation has a number of unacceptable side-effects. The rise and rise of the global economy is one of the great achievements of the late twentieth century. The forging together of a single world market for a growing number of goods and services is equated with an upward improvement in the standard of living of everyone – first world and third world citizens alike. The linking together of markets, companies and cities in a global web in which capital has an unfettered flow is widely considered a unanimous success. The creation of a so-called global village with global citizens is regarded as part of this convergence and homogenisation of prosperity. The liberalisation of capital labour markets, and trade barriers, has yielded gains in the efficiency of the economic systems. It has rewarded corporations with burgeoning sales, turnover and profits. And for the consumer, improved quality of services and goods, increasingly sophisticated consumer gadgets and lower prices.

Liberalisation also can be given some credit for driving the convergence of economies with the EU. Take, for instance, gross domestic product per head: a measure of a country's prosperity. If we compare GDP per head for three of Europe's poorest countries – Spain, Portugal and Ireland – against Germany (the EU's richest nation) between 1970 and 1990 all three increased their prosperity relative to Germany.

However, the severe social and human consequences of the liberalisation have not been considered on the same balance sheet as these economic benefits. The continuation of liberalisation of markets calls into question the long-term efficacy of economic systems as we know them today.

The extent and global nature of the side-effects of liberalisation are serious. The International Labour Organisation estimates that there is a higher proportion of people unemployed in the world today than at any other time since the 1930s. Some 30 per cent of the global workforce are either unemployed or under-employed. Put another way, about 820 million people are unemployed[13]. Although some scepticism needs to placed on this measure – the records of the 1930s are both sketchy and do not reflect today's level of industrialisation – the global consequences of liberalisation and globalisation are huge.

Contrary to popular belief, what we have seen over the last 30 years has been a growing mismatch in prosperity – a widening global divide between rich and poor. With the expansion and integration of the world economy has been an equally powerful force, that of the growing gap between the prosperous and the disadvantaged. It is estimated by the United Nations that the ratio of income shares between the world's poorest 20 per cent and the world's richest 20 per cent has risen from 30:1 in 1960 to 61:1[14].

The spread of poverty is, however, very uneven. A glimpse of the distribution of poverty across the world's major regions shows growing differences. The engine of the global economy – South East Asia – shows a narrowing gap over the last decade in the proportion of the population below the poverty line, according to UN data. The picture in Latin America and Africa is less encouraging. In both these regions the level of poverty has increased over the last ten years. Indeed, United Nations forecasts estimate that the percentage of the population below the poverty line will grow. A further measure of the emerging disparity can be gauged by the fact that sales of the world's four largest TNCs – General Motors, Ford, Exxon, and Shell – exceed the gross national product of all Africa.

Part of the problem obviously stems from the transition that developed economies are currently undergoing; making the shift from producing low-value-added goods and services into high-technology manufacturing and high-quality-service industries. The effect in developed economies has been one that has displaced low-skill workers, and increased the demand for highly skilled ones. As we have already discussed, the key imperative driving change is the difference that exists in wage costs. But it is not only low wage costs.

The ravage of unemployment and poverty is not only isolated to the developing world, it also is severe in Europe: showing that globalisation is increasingly not just an economic, but also a social phenomenon. The unemployed rate in the EU in 1993 was eleven per cent, whereas in the 1960s it averaged two per cent[15]. This burden is a growing drag on the competitiveness of Europe in the international economy; this is an economic and social illness that needs to be treated. It is also a major cause of the growing government debt of many European economies and precipitated the collapse of the exchange rate mechanism in 1992.

Perhaps most worrying is the growing polarisation across the EU. Again using unemployment as a measure, Table 2.5 illustrates this growing divide. A look at the national average rates shows a relatively homogenous picture, with the exception of Spain. The majority of countries fall between Germany at 4.5 per cent and Britain with an average unemployment rate of 10.8 per cent. However, this even spread masks sharp disparities at a regional level, in two ways. First, within each nation state the regional differences are marked. Take middle ranking Belgium: the worst region has a jobless rate

Table 2.5 A divided Europe (unemployment rates in 1992, %)

	National Average	Regional Range
Belgium	8.2	5.6–10.8
Germany	4.5	2.9–7.7
Greece	7.7	4.8–9.9
Spain	18.0	12.5–25.9
France	10.0	8.0–12.9
Italy	10.3	4.2–21.8
Portugal	4.8	3.7–4.5
Netherlands	6.7	6.3–8.5
Britain	10.8	8.3–16.7

Source: European Commission 'Eurostat' (1994)

about double that of the most successful region. Second, this trend is also replicated across Europe: between the jobless blackspot of Spain's worst region at nearly 26 per cent, to Germany's lowest region at about 3 per cent.

The rise in jobless totals across Europe has run parallel to the introduction of free markets in Europe. As we have already seen the privatisation and injection of competition into former state monopolies has resulted in huge job losses. For instance, in France privatised firms have been no better than public enterprises in preserving jobs: some 136 000 jobs have been shed since 1983 by Bull, Aerospatiale, Renault, Ugine-Sacilor, Thomsen and Pechiney – all privatised companies.

This chapter has illustrated the way that the ideology of the market has radically changed economic activity. The managed process of liberalisation within GATT gave market forces momentum to bring about globalisation. This momentum forged the global economy out of a set of different and disparate trade blocs. In doing so, it brought a new pressure to bear on Europe. In the past Europe had been embedded in regulation, restrictive practices and state intervention. Europe had to respond to the pressures of globalisation by introducing its own round of liberalisation, to retain global competitiveness.

However, liberalisation also hit at the heart of Euro-capitalism. Liberalisation has exposed the beautiful quality of life of Europeans, to the ugly forces of global competition, so that Europe now stands at a cross-roads in its history. The signpost suggests there are two routes. The first involves relaxing the progressive agenda to modernise Europe, and points to a fortress Europe. A Europe in which the quality of life will be maintained, but living standards will continue their long-term decline. The alternative path involves further liberalisation, but holds up the opportunity of longer-term prosperity. However, although this route is undoubtedly better, it comes with a warning. Excessive liberalisation threatens not only the efficiency and effectiveness of European economies, but also the prosperity of Europe.

Notes

1.   *The Economist* (1993) GATT: The eleventh hour. 4 December p. 25.

2. International Labour Organisation (1995) *World Employment Report*. ILO. Geneva.

3. *The Economist* (1993) GATT: The eleventh hour. 4 December p. 25.

4. Kenichi Ohmae (1990) *The borderless world: Power and strategy in the interlinked economy*. Harper Perennial. New York, p.94.

5. Adrian Hamilton (1986) *The financial revolution*. Penguin. London, p. 13.

6. Hamish McRae (1993) *The world in 2010*. Harper Collins. London.

7. R. Thomas (1995) Institutional themes on jobless variations. *The Guardian* 20 February p. 11. Data from UNCTAD.

8. World Bank (1989) *World Development Report*. Word Bank. Washington DC.

9. Peter Dicken (1992) *Global Shift*. Paul Chapman. London.

10. A. Amin, D. Charles and J. Howells (1992) Corporate Restructuring and the Single Market. Regional Studies.

11. Although some 11 000 of these firms were in the former East Germany. The sums of capital involved have been equally as massive: some $328 billion between 1985 and 1992. Banque Paribas (1995) Conjuncture: Privatisation February No. 2. Paris.

12. According to estimates by Morgan Stanley, a US investment bank.

13. International Labour Organisation (1995) *World Employment Report*. ILO. Geneva.

14. United Nations (1994) *World Investment Report*. UNCTAD. Geneva.

15. H.M. Treasury (1994) Economic Briefing: Unemployment No. 7 October. HMSO. London.

3 European Financial Services

INTRODUCTION

Firms of all sizes across the European market face a new challenge in an era after liberalisation. The completion of the single market means that capital and labour, goods and services are moving with greater freedom. As a result, powerful forces are now at work that will dissolve national regulatory barriers that have preserved the structure, concentration and stolidness of European industry. This is particularly true in the financial services industry, where the liberal reforms of the single market process are beginning to drive a change from a set of national self-contained financial systems to a single, interconnected financial market. Consequently, the convergence of financial systems that is at hand, is placing formerly national financial organisations at a strategic crossroads. As the end of the decade draws to a close, the question for all financial service companies is which route to follow?

This chapter examines the different liberalising forces at work that are bringing European financial services to this historical point. Three main trends are identified as being at the heart of this change. First the revolutionary changes, which swept through the international financial system during the 1980s, are in the 1990s acting to integrate the formerly separate financial systems of the EU15[1]. The second factor has evolved symbolically, in that governments and the European Commission (EC) have initiated changes in the rules that regulate markets, in particular financial markets. Third, EU governments are privatising vast tracts of state-owned financial services to inject competition, to reduce public deficits and to rollback the frontiers of the state. Together these three developments are carrying forward the pace of integration and are resulting in the convergence of European financial systems.

In general European monetary systems have been cosseted for the last 40 years by state control and regulation. Segmented market structures created by regulation have isolated financial institutions from competition. Many financial organisations became bloated on the profits of cartels.

The introduction of competition into the financial services industry would – according to the seminal Cecchini study[2] – have massive potential benefits for Europe by: *'catalysing the economy as a whole. Removal of barriers here, and of the costs linked to them would lead to three interlocking effects: a surge in the competitiveness of the sector itself; a knock-on boost to all businesses using its increasingly efficient services, and more generally a new and positive influence on the conduct of macro-economic policy in the EU'.* Cecchini estimated that the gains from the liberalisation of financial services would produce direct economic benefits of 22 billion Ecu (1985 prices) equivalent to 27.5 per cent to 33.8 per cent of the total economic gain from the completion of the Single European Market. These benefits have yet to be fully accrued, but the magnitude of the figures demonstrates the powerful economic forces unleashed by liberalisation of financial services.

A key consequence of the deregulation of financial services means that Europe in the late 1990s will be characterised by a period of sectoral, inter-sectoral and organisational restructuring. The intensification of competition between financial institutions within financial markets will eat into profits and so drive a process of innovation, as financial institutions engage in a search for new profit-making opportunities, driving further competitive deregulation. As a result firms will seek a competitive advantage through new organisational structures. The strategic path taken will be highly individualistic to each company. The signpost to success will be based on a strategy tailored to the challenge of converging European markets in the next century.

THE GLOBAL FINANCIAL SYSTEM AND THE FORMATION OF THE EUROPEAN MONETARY SYSTEM

The 1980s were witness to major transformations of the international political, economic, and financial environment. Among the major developments was rapidly increasing international financial integration across financial major nations and across financial

*product markets. The major sources of financial change were several,
inter-related and reinforcing.[3]*

The convergence of financial systems within the EU must be
viewed from the changes that have transformed the landscape
of the international financial system. The institutional and
regulatory controls that characterise the financial systems of
today are largely a product of the financial crisis of the 1930s.
Prior to this crisis, the world financial system had been based
around the mutually sustaining factors of Britain's economic
superiority – free-trade and the gold standard – which were
almost completely co-ordinated by activities in London's
financial markets.

The economic depression, precipitated by the Wall Street
Crash of 1929, flooded quickly into other sectors of the world
economy. It was in the knowledge of these possibilities that
governments and the finance industry compartmentalised
financial markets to limit the damage to other areas of the
financial and economic system during a period of crisis. The
key element of this international economic co-ordination was
the Bretton Woods Accord, which pegged all participating
currencies to the dollar. This system produced international
economic instability by providing liquidity to finance
temporary deficits in the international system. These multi-
national institutional structures supported national regulatory
financial regimes in Europe, in particular by discouraging
trade in capital.

The demise of this system in the early 1970s was caused by
the inflexibility of the system, which prevented it from
adjusting to the dynamism of capital flows. The ending of the
accord enabled the rapid globalisation of capital, placing
international and national regimes under further stress to
liberalise financial markets and remove the long-standing
barriers to trade in financial services. These have been
characterised by trends towards the breakdown in the
segmentation of financial markets, national markets becoming
increasingly integrated internationally, and almost everywhere
competition in financial markets has intensified.

The financial revolution of the 1980s – described in Chapter
2 – has resulted in a new financial landscape. This landscape
was shaped by deregulation and technology, which together

stimulated financial innovation. It was also shaped by the continued ideological shift to market-forces. In short, the erosion of regulation and the fusion of computer and telecommunications inter-connected the formerly separate financial markets in North America, Asia and Europe into a global marketplace for capital.

The emerging free-market for capital left governments to cope with free-floating currencies. In the face of increased currency volatility came the idea of tying Europe's currencies closer together, to bring economic stability back to Europe. This was a journey that would culminate in the Maastricht Treaty some two decades later.

THE ROAD TO ECONOMIC AND MONETARY UNION

Economic instability in the 1970s brought down the regulatory structures of an earlier era. The institutions established by Bretton Woods were now incapable of meeting the new challenges of growing volatility in the world economy. It was in this context that the members of the then EEC decided to band together to enhance economic integration. At the same time, the EC had initiated the Werner Report of 1970, which set out the objectives of closer union. The Werner Report recommended that goods and services, people and capital should be able to circulate freely in Europe. The events that led up to the Maastricht Treaty and closer co-ordination of exchange rates are outlined in Table 3.1.

The first attempt by the EEC to stabilise the exchange rates was termed the *snake*, since it was envisaged that European currencies would move in line with each other. The *snake* lasted only one year, and was abandoned in favour of floating exchange rates. The external economic pressures on Europe at this time, such as the 1973 oil crisis, prevented the Werner Report from being implemented. In spite of the failure of the *snake*, the experience of co-operation resulted in the formation of the European Monetary System (EMS) in 1979. This had the specific aim of creating 'a zone of monetary stability in Europe'. In general, the formation of the EMS marked a change in macro-economic policy with the shift to manage inflation via monetary control. As part of the EMS, the

Table 3.1 A brief history of monetary convergence in Europe

Date	Event
1972	European currency snake created. Belgium, Denmark, Norway, West Germany, Britain, Italy and France link their currencies to the US dollar
March 1979	European Monetary System and exchange rate mechanism established
June 1987	France devalues and declares a policy of Franc fort
July 1990	Bundesbank forced to swap Deutschmarks for ostmarks at one-for-one
October 1990	Britain joins ERM
December 1991	Treaty on Economic and Monetary Union signed by the 12 members of the EU, agreeing a move to a single currency by 1999 at the latest
June 1992	Danes reject Maastricht Treaty
September 1992	EU finance ministers reject realignment of ERM. Britain and Italy leave ERM. Portugal and Spain devalue currency
August 1993	Effective dismantling of ERM, with widening of currency bands to 15%

Source: *The Observer* 1 August 1993: author's own observations

exchange rate mechanism was established to reduce currency fluctuations and enhance inflationary control.

By the 1980s, the relative success of this system and the increasing pace of the European integration process, embodied in the single market programme (see below), prompted the EC to produce the Delors Report on economic and monetary union (EMU). It recommended that the process of EMU should take place in four stages. The centrepiece of Stage 1 was the Exchange Rate Mechanism (ERM). Stage 2 officially began on 1 January 1994, with the set-up of the European Monetary Institute, the fledgling European central bank in Frankfurt. Stage 3 also set down four criteria that have to be met by the majority of member states (Table 3.2), before a single currency can be introduced in Stage 4 by 1999. The process of EMU has been necessitated by the creation of the single European market. It is the completion of the unified market in January 1993, and the creation of the European financial area with the freeing of capital movements that has and will continue to be the driving force in European financial services.

Table 3.2 Maastricht convergence criteria

Four recommended economic criteria are included in the Maastricht Treaty to achieve Economic and Monetary Union in 1997 or 1999 if the majority of EU countries meet the criteria

---

Stage 1. Each member state must attain an average rate of inflation that does not exceed the average inflation rate of the best performing three states by more than 1.5 per cent.

Stage2. The ratio of government deficit to gross domestic product (GDP) cannot exceed 3 per cent and the ratio of government debt cannot exceed 60 per cent.

Stage 3. In the year before entering into EMU a country's average nominal long-term interest rates may not exceed the average of the best performing member states by more than 2 per cent.

Stage 4. In the 2 years preceding admission to the EMU, the currency of each member state must remain within the 2.25 per cent band of fluctuation in the ERM.

Source: L. Hatheway (1992) One European Financial Market *UBS International Finance* Winter Issue 14, 1–8

THE SINGLE EUROPEAN MARKET AND LIBERALISATION

The liberalisation of capital movements and of financial services is an indispensable element in the realisation of the large European internal market.[4]

Throughout the last 20 years, the notion of liberalising economic activity has gained increasing credence. The liberalisation of financial services has been at the heart of the creation of a single market. There have been two components of change that have been especially significant in the deregulation of financial services in Europe. The first is the geographical liberalisation with regard to financial institutions' cross-border movements and the deregulation of the supply of financial services that has resulted from directives with the single market programme. The second has to do with the liberalisation of capital flows between EU countries. These two aspects are central to the functioning of the unified market in aiding the free movement of goods, services, labour, and capital: the stated aim of the SEM.

Using the example of the banking industry, it is possible to trace the introduction of financial liberalisation. It was first initiated in the EU by the passing of the First Banking Directive in 1977. This directive, which applied to banking institutions, established minimum requirements for the authorisation and supervision of these institutions. Two criteria were applied under this directive: a minimum capital level within every institution, and an 'honest', experienced management. In effect, most countries in the EU had at this time stricter regulations than set-down in this directive. Hence, a number of differences remained between the banking systems of member states.

With the initiation of the single market process in the mid-1980s, the ultimate objective of the EC was to remove all barriers which impeded free-trade in financial services. Hence the principle of mutual recognition in financial markets was adopted. This principle operates by the premise of home country control which allows a bank to set up in any member state under the regulation of its home country: in effect giving it a single passport to operate anywhere in the single market. It was the adoption of this principle that marked the definitive turning point in the convergence of financial sectors throughout the EU. Mutual recognition means that the ongoing process of integration will take place across the EU through competitive deregulation.

The principle of mutual recognition was first introduced in the Second Banking Directive in 1986. This directive sets out the idea of the single passport, which permits any bank – or other financial institution – to offer a range of banking services in any other member state under the basis of only one licence. This was a very important step because it permitted further financial integration without excessively expanding the body of existing regulations. By implication, these directives will result in the future integration of the financial systems, sectors and institutions.

The second aspect of the internal market programme of key significance to the liberalisation of financial systems is the freeing of capital markets. This directive, adopted in 1988, enables the free movement of capital across the EU. The impetus for this change was the increasing volume of capital flowing in the international financial system. Britain was the first to abolish exchange controls in 1979, but was quickly followed throughout the 1980s by Germany, France, the Netherlands, Denmark, Belgium, Luxembourg and Italy. The directive also allowed Spain, Ireland, Portugal and Greece until the end of 1992 to abolish exchange controls.

Without this directive it would not have been possible to achieve the free trade in financial services and the eradication of the barriers impeding capital flows. With its introduction, member states lost control over flows of money in and out of their financial system, placing even greater strain on their credit and monetary policies. In essence, a European single financial market now exists. For individuals and companies alike are free to invest and borrow in any area of the EU. The implications are that capital is now free to move anywhere in the EU driven only by market forces. The resulting convergence of financial systems has placed a heavy burden on financial services to restructure market operations to meet both competition of new entrants and new flows of capital in their financial system. An overview of the European retail banking industry illustrates the impact of these liberalisation forces.

THE CHANGING STRUCTURE OF EUROPEAN FINANCIAL SERVICES

The relic that the Bretton Woods Accord left behind was the raft of regulatory controls on European financial markets. Financial regulation existed in all countries for similar micro-economic reasons. First, to provide a payments mechanism, which facilitates the transfer of money between individuals and companies. Second, to supply a variety of financial services to customers to support deposit facilities and advanced credit operations. Third, financial intermediaries brought savers and borrowers together, which reduced risk within the monetary system.

The importance of the financial sector to all member states of the EU has increased throughout the 1980s; the industry is a major employer. Throughout the 1980s employment

Table 3.3 The retail banking industry in the EU (data for 1989)

	No. of Banks	No. of Branches	No. of Employees
France	1 000	25 480	409 350
Germany	4 379	61 940	604 000
Italy	232	9 684	210 390
Spain	342	33 433	237 181
Britain	180	8 990	408 182

Source: A. Llado, A. Garcia, M. Soler and J. Isern (1989) *Los sistemas bancarios de los principales paises de la CEE* Caxia de Pensions, Barcelona. C. Gentle (1993) *The Financial Services*, Avebury, Aldershot. Britain Banking Abstracts (1992)

increased across Europe, with Luxembourg and Britain showing particularly large increases. In total almost 1.6 million people are employed in financial services throughout the EU. The majority of these are employed in Europe's core economies: Germany, Britain, France, Italy and Spain. Within each of these economies financial services account for over 2.5 per cent of total employment.[5]

Currently, financial services is a relatively fragmented industry both within member states and on a European basis. Table 3.3 illustrates the different structures of banking across Europe's major economies. The first point to note is that it is very difficult to make comparisons across these figures, since very different regulatory structures have been adopted across the EU. For instance, Germany has the most branches due to its federal banking structure and a high number of local savings banks. By contrast, Britain has relatively fewer banks and branches in its retail banking sector. This is due to the centralised nature of its financial markets and the greater degree of competition.

A similar picture is illustrated by Table 3.4, which shows significant differences in market share held by major players in the banking industry across Europe. These differences can be explained again by the regulatory patchwork that characterises Europe, but also by the level of state control. In France, for instance, the majority of major banks were in state control until the early 1990s, leading to the high degree of concentration.

The banking sector has evolved in very different ways across

Table 3.4 Market concentration in the banking industry in Europe (1989)

	Largest 3	Largest 5	Largest 10
France	36.1	54.5	71.4
Germany	15.3	26.1	37.0
Italy	19.5	36.2	48.7
Spain	30.2	38.5	64.7
Britain	22.5	29.2	42.2

Source: J. Canals (1993) *Competitive Strategies in European Banking* OUP, Oxford

the EU. It has been shaped in each country by the mix of regulatory controls (both private and state imposed), technological applications, and cultural factors. It is evident that the broad trend with European financial services over the coming years will be the demise of the highly structured and regulated financial systems of the passing era, and the emergence of a more competitive Europe-wide financial system. The implications of a convergence of financial sectors in Europe will result in significant corporate reorganisation. This will be driven by liberalisation, privatisation, and deregulation.

THE CONVERGENCE OF FINANCIAL SYSTEMS WILL BE DRIVEN BY CORPORATE REORGANISATION

It is clear that major changes are coming over the horizon for the structure of individual financial systems throughout the EU. The key to understanding this process is the changing structure and strategies adopted by large banks, insurers and financial conglomerates. The coming together of the liberalisation of financial services and restructuring within large financial institutions is driving the European financial market towards convergence. The dynamic underpinning this change is that of competition. The European financial services industry is on the brink of a period of competitive deregulation. Meanwhile, across the EU large financial institutions are already rapidly reorganising their structure and redefining strategies in order to meet the challenge of an increase in competition.

It is the unleashing of the dynamism of competition that will be the key force in the formation of the European financial area. Prior to the implementation of the single market directives, the financial sector in many member states was segmented by regulation. This partitioning also meant that there was no direct competition between financial institutions operating in separate areas of the financial system. This situation also prevented financial institutions from engaging in the process of financial innovation: defined as the process by which financial institutions develop new financial instruments, enabling them to move outside existing regulatory frameworks and into new markets.

The liberalisation of the international financial system has resulted in competition seeping into national financial systems. Once the level of competition within financial markets intensifies, then financial institutions will seek to further free themselves from the shackles of regulation. This point has been reached in only a few EU states, notably Britain which in part sought to improve its macro-economic position through liberalisation. However, once this threshold of competition has been reached, the intensification of competition between financial institutions will grow apace. Thus further reducing profitability and, in turn, firing further competition.

In order to maintain profitability, financial institutions are being driven into the process of financial innovation. The strategy adopted to realise any profitable opportunities from innovations by financial companies in Britain has been diversification into new markets. In turn, financial institutions have reappraised and reconfigured the structure and strategy of their organisation.

Clearly, the situation in Europe is more complex than that argued above. In that it is not possible to identify the same process underway at the same time throughout the different regions of the EU. In particular, this results from the very different financial systems in place across the EU. Nonetheless, the key point is that the introduction of competition has opened up national markets, both to domestic and EU competition. This means that financial organisations are arriving at an important crossroads: forced on them by the process of competitive deregulation. But one which will result in a prolonged period of sectoral, inter-sectoral and organisational restructuring in the future, which will bind the formerly separate markets of Europe into a single financial market.

This process is already underway. Take for instance the acquisitive activities of large financial firms over recent years. Since the mid-1980s corporate restructuring has been taking place via cross-border alliances; national alliances; and cross-border mergers and acquisitions. There are five points to note about this process.

First, the number of merger and acquisition deals has been greater than the number of agreements forged between institutions undertaking co-operative ways of reorganising for the single market. This is because many financial institutions were driven on by the spectre of the growth of other (large) potential competitors in other member states.

Second, some mergers and acquisitions involved companies which operated within the confines of the domestic market. In a similar way to cross-border mergers and acquisitions, many firms reacted to the potential for large firms to encroach into their home markets. As a result larger financial firms have acquired smaller domestic firms. In general, these changes have taken place in countries with heavy regulatory controls and/or with smaller, lighter capitalised institutions. Such concentration of corporate power has taken place in Italy, Denmark, and the Netherlands. For instance, in Italy the low levels of competition have resulted from the heavy compartmentalisation of the financial system. The need to improve the cost-effectiveness, customer service and (international) competitiveness, has resulted in much (state sponsored) merger and acquisitive activity.

Third, on an international scale most merger and acquisition activity has been characterised by large financial institutions buying smaller firms. This type of restructuring has, in general, taken place between firms in different areas of the financial sector. For instance, the acquisition by Deutsche Bank of two merchant banks (Morgan Grenfell in Britain, and MDM in Portugal).

Fourth, links forged between large financial institutions have mostly taken place on an international scale, by striking alliances and co-operative agreements. This has in many cases involved the exchange of equity or capital, so as to guard against being acquired by other firms and to gain a foothold in

Table 3.5 European privatisation banking candidates

Bank	Country	Govt holding %	Value $m
Creditanstalt	Austria	49.3	930
Bank Austria	Austria	21.7	1032
Credit Lyonnais	France	54.0	2346
Credit Local	France	25.5	728
BNP	France	73.0	5038
Credito Italiano	Italy	67.0	877
Crediop	Italy	51.0	N/A
Banca Commerciale Italiano	Italy	57.0	2182
Instituto Mobiliare Italiano	Italy	100.0	N/A
Banca di Roma	Italy	86.9	2101
Banco di Napoli	Italy	13.0	570
Den Norsk	Norway	70.0	1520
Christiana	Norway	100.0	N/A
Banco Portuges do Atlantico	Portugal	23.0	330
Banco Pinto	Portugal	100.0	N/A
Argentaria	Spain	75.0	3442
Nordbanken	Sweden	100.0	2510
Gotabank	Sweden	100.0	800

Source: Morgan Stanley Bank

another EU country. For example, the deal between Banco Santander (Spain) and the Royal Bank of Scotland (Britain).

Finally, it should be noted that the number of firms available for acquisition has been limited. This is because many governments have been apprehensive about letting domestic banks fall into the hands of foreign companies. However, with the increase in privatisation that is taking place, the number of institutions available for acquisition will rise dramatically (Table 3.5).

SUMMARY

It is clear from this chapter that there are radical changes taking place in the form and structure of European financial services. It is also evident that, as yet, it is hard to define a European financial market evolving from the considerable corporate turmoil. Nonetheless, there is a general trend in Europe of moving away from highly structured and closely regulated national financial systems, towards increasingly deregulated and competitive financial sectors closely inter-linked with the liberalisation of international financial markets. The changes have gone furthest in Britain, where governments have encouraged them, than in Germany, for example, where governments have put up more resistance, but the basic pattern can be seen everywhere.

This chapter has followed the liberalising events that are leading to the formation of the European financial market from the post-war Bretton Woods Accord. The emergence of an international financial system resulted from the demise of Bretton Woods. More importantly, it initiated regulatory change in Europe. The adoption by governments of liberalis-ing policies resulted in an era of deregulation throughout European economies. The EC, in recognising this trend, introduced its internal market programme, using the prin-ciples of a single passport and mutual recognition to create a process of competitive deregulation.

This chapter has shown how, over the next decade, the pace of regulatory change across the EU will quicken. The liberalisation of European financial services using the principle of mutual harmonisation is leading to a convergence of financial systems across the EU; thus removing the barriers that have held national financial systems apart from each other. For financial institutions this will result in a prolonged period of sectoral, inter-sectoral and organisational restructuring. By early in the next century a unified financial market will exist, creating a significant force that will shape Europe in the twenty-first century.

Notes

1. CEC (1988) *A European Financial Area: the liberalisation of capital movements*. CEC. Luxembourg.
2. P. Cecchini (1988) *The European Challenge 1992*. Wildhouse. Aldershot, p. 37.
3. F. Edwards and H. T. Patrick (1992) *Regulating International Financial Markets*. Kluwer. Massachusetts, p. 2.
4. CEC (1988) *A European Financial Area: the liberalisation of capital movements*. CEC. Luxembourg, p. 3.
5. J. Canals (1993) *Competitive Strategies in European Banking*. OUP. Oxford.

4 European Computer Services

INTRODUCTION

Although the computer services industry[1] is seen as an increasingly significant sector of activity in terms of technological development and competitive advantage, its strategic and policy value within Europe has always been underplayed. This may have been for a number of reasons relating to preconceptions about the industry: it was seen as following technological developments in the wider information technology (IT) industry. As a 'service' activity, its locational distribution was also seen to closely reflect the distribution of demand via the need for close customer contact, language and cultural factors: local demand was met by local supply. In turn, as a reflection, trade in computer services was low, with one estimate in the mid-1980s putting domestic demand accounting for 90 per cent or more of the market[2].

As a consequence, although the computer services market within the European Union (EU) has been estimated to be 33.5 billion Ecu in 1989, and employing 350 000 people[3], it has not held much significance within the European Commission (EC), member states or regional development agencies. This situation is now changing, with the recognition that there is a higher degree of value-added associated with computer services and software.

This chapter seeks to re-evaluate and redress some of the old preconceptions about the industry and to highlight its size, continuing growth prospects, and economic and technological significance within the EU. It seeks to focus on the changing nature of the industry, which has evolved in often subtle ways. Thus it outlines the way that the industry is responding to the new challenge of European integration, within the wider global framework, and considers how this is affecting the organisational development of the industry.

MARKET GROWTH AND CHANGE IN EUROPEAN COMPUTER SERVICES

Since the mid-1980s the IT industry has been characterised by the need to develop complete business solutions incorporating both hardware and software applications, and has been reflected in the growth of the systems integration market.

This evolutionary path has resulted in dramatic growth rates both in the number of computer services companies and in their size. This new phase of development in computer services is taking place within the wider context of a marked slowdown in the rate of growth in the world and European IT markets. Thus, in 1991 the world IT market grew by only 4.1 per cent compared to 18.1 per cent in 1987; whilst the European market actually recorded a decline of 17.2 per cent between 1990 and 1991. These figures provide some suggestion that the IT industry is becoming more mature, especially over the last few years (Table 4.1).

A disaggregation of the different segments of the global IT revenues indicates that the computer services and software segments have continued to be the most dynamic sectors of the industry (Table 4.2). Over the last few years, growth rates of over 40 per cent between 1987 and 1991 can be compared to major declines in every hardware sector except personal computers (PCs).

As such electronic systems have become ever more sophisticated, demand for software has grown ever more rapid. This is not a recently charted phenomenon however. The often quoted S-curve figure of the hardware/software cost ratio has

Table 4.1 Global IT revenues 1987–91[1] ($ billions)

	1987	1989	1991
Europe	37.0	37.8	34.6
N. America	134.0	157.0	175.4
Rest of World	37.9	61.0	80.0
Total	208.9	255.8	290.0

[1] These figures are compiled from Top 100 IT corporation.

Source: *Datamation* 15 June 1991; 15 June 1992; 1 July 1992

After Liberalisation

Table 4.2 Global IT markets (1987 and 1991)

| | % Global Revenue | | % Change |
	1987	1991	'87–'91
Large Scale Systems	12.6	9.5	–24.6
Midrange	10.7	7.6	–29.0
PCs	10.6	15.2	+43.4
Workstations	4.7	—	
Peripherals	25.0	20.9	–16.4
Data Communications	7.1	5.3	–25.3
Software	8.1	11.5	+42.0
Computer Services	7.6	11.0	+44.7
Maintenance	13.0	11.1	–14.6
Other	5.3	3.2	–39.6

Source: adapted from *Datamation* 15 June 1992

in the past suggested that the relative share of software costs to hardware costs in IT applications will continue to rise over time.

However, what is significant now is that software and computer service sales have now become larger than hardware sales in many major industrial economies. In Britain, hardware and data communication sales totalled $8 867 million compared with computer service and software sales of $9 682 million[4].

Aside from the actual growth in the size and significance of computer services, there is another set of changes which is having a major impact on the structure and nature of the industry. These changes appear to be coalescing together and suggest that the industry within Europe may be at a watershed in its development. They relate to:

1. Increasing competition within hardware manufacturing, leading to diversification by computer manufacturers into services and software.
2. A trend towards the internationalisation of the industry associated with widening (geographical) market expansion and competition.

3. The move by computer service companies to offer a 'one-stop shop' to their major clients (product market expansion).
4. The creation of the Single European Market.
5. The liberalisation of public procurement restrictions.

These trends have hit hardest in the hardware sector. Hardware manufacturers face increasing competitive pressures in three areas. One, in association with the continued long-term decline in the basic price of computers. Two, the rising cost of research and development. Three, the creation of more open competitive markets associated with the gradual demise of non-interoperable standards and the adoption of UNIX and open systems. As a consequence the profitability of hardware manufacture has continued to fall. For example, IBM restructured its global operations via the formation of 23 alliance companies and shed 180 000 jobs world-wide by 1992 and a further 100 000 jobs were cut after the company recorded the largest ever corporate loss in history – $4.9 billion – in 1992[5].

Not unexpectedly, companies involved in hardware manufacture have sought to expand their related computer service activities where companies have been able to maintain high margins. IBM has been a prime example of this and by 1991 claimed that 43 per cent ($28 billion) of its $64.8 billion revenues came from computer service and related activities[6]. This move has been achieved both through organic growth and via acquisition activity.

A second factor which is leading to major changes in the industry is the globalisation of computer service companies. On the demand side, key customers of these companies, the major TNCs as they themselves have globalised, have found it increasingly unsatisfactory dealing with several different computer service companies for their operations scattered across the various continents. As a result, major computer service companies have been pressed to offer software development, support and maintenance facilities across the EU. However, this has brought a competitive advantage which they can use to attract other internationally based customers to use their services. Both Cap Gemini Sogeti and EDS have attested to this in their drive for global coverage. A related factor here is that of the pressure for product diversification, where key customers have sought a 'one-stop shop' in terms of their computer service needs.

On the supply side, competition in computer services is appearing globally from a number of new sources. The Japanese, who have traditionally been seen as weak in terms of software generation, are now producing high quality software efficiently. A key element in this has been Japan's new software factories which, although copied from US competitors such as IBM and TRW, are now evolving much more advanced systems in strategic management and economies of scope in software production. However, more recently commentators have sought to downplay the Japanese threat due to their orientation towards writing bespoke software for a small number of very large domestic corporate customers using mainframe computers[7]. This market has suffered considerable retrenchment in recent years, causing heavy losses in a number of formerly fast-growing Japanese software companies. Another competitive threat is from less developed countries who are increasingly providing quality software services at extremely low cost, often supported by government policy in terms of import restrictions and incentives. Thus Singapore has encouraged the establishment of software centres by DEC, Unisys and Hewlett Packard. Similarly in India, the indigenous state-owned company CMC has won contracts in overseas countries, such as providing software for London Underground and La Suisse Insurance. Similarly, foreign companies operating in India, such as Bull and BT in a joint venture with a local software company Mahindra, are using the country as a low cost software base to compete for European and US business[8].

A prime example of globalisation of service provision has been EDS which has acquired a series of companies, including the major acquisition of SD-Scicon in Britain, in order to broaden its product portfolio to satisfy its major corporate customers. Figure 4.1 outlines diversification moves by other key players in the computer services industry in order to meet client needs. In addition, these patterns of diversification are also being driven by the desire of large companies to move into the consultancy and the implementation stage of software development. This is an attempt to add more value to their services, but also to be in a position to 'roll-out' contracts

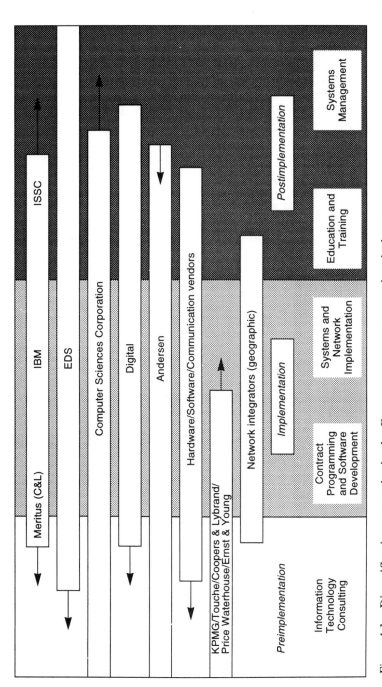

Figure 4.1 Diversification strategies in the European computer services industry

Source: International Data Corporation, 1992

through implementation and systems management stages. This strategy is particularly important within the current environment where large multinationals are looking for two or three long-term global suppliers for their IT software and services needs.

Within Europe the globalisation of service provision and supply developments has stimulated the creation of the Single European Market (SEM). A key development that has flowed from the SEM has been the liberalisation of public procurement practices, that have in the past hindered non-domestic computer service operators from gaining key contracts from national and local governments, large utilities and major state companies. In the context of the creation of the SEM, their gradual removal has further encouraged the emergence of pan-European computer service operations. Not only are key customers therefore seeking to establish more integrated cross-border production and service operators, but computer service companies now face fewer restrictions and more opportunities in developing a more co-ordinated European operation. Companies such as CGS, EDS (owned by General Motors) and Andersen Consulting are building up European networks where particular countries take the lead for particular product lines. To underwrite this 'one-stop' provision of service, large computer service firms have established centres of excellence[9].

The issue of public procurement has been closely related to European legislation on the Single Market and the need for 'open' markets. In the 1970s and 1980s, when the industry was in its primacy, a number of companies benefited from state procured contracts within their closed domestic market. Two examples of the importance of these contracts are the domestic markets of France and Italy. In France, the industry has been a principal benefactor of state schemes such as the Minitel project and the Transpac network. French companies, such as Cap Gemini Sogeti, have used such contracts as a base to internationalise their services. A similar position has been replicated in Italy, in particular Finsiel (part of the state holding company IRI) has had a stable, non-competitive market of state enterprises to use as a platform of growth. However, the awarding of a major European Commission contract to the Japanese owned ICL, suggests that future procurement from Brussels will not simply favour European-owned firms. Public procured contracts have in the past helped to sustain a number of strong domestic companies, some of which are now beginning to expand into other member state markets. All these forces are therefore fusing together to refashion the European computer services industry.

THE INDUSTRY RESPONSE: CONSOLIDATION, RATIONALISATION AND STRATEGIC PARTNERSHIP IN EUROPE

What are the implications of these changes on the European computer services industry? A key element here is that a gradual decline of national markets and players is apparent and that indeed it is becoming increasingly applicable to talk about a European rather than, for example, a Spanish or French industry. A trend that can be identified in this period of sectoral, inter-sectoral and organisational change is that the industry in Europe is undergoing a period of restructuring. Prior to this period, five key factors were important in sustaining such a national orientation. These were:

1. Public procurement.
2. Language has been a crucial part of market segmentation within European computer services and especially the software market, because of programming difficulties. As pan-European computer-based service companies have been established, language has tended to be a key factor in the design of their pan-European corporate structures.
3. Dominance of national hardware suppliers with the peculiarities of their own operating systems – now disappearing with the emergence of open systems and the disappearance of 'national champions'.
4. National standards and certification – again these are now eroding but were a key factor in national market segmentation.
5. Size – and geographical scope – has only now become a major factor as multinational customers encourage geographical and product market diversification to support their needs.

These factors, which previously allowed considerable advantages to domestic computer service players, are now increasingly being eroded. Thus, it is harder for governments to show favouritism in handing out contracts to national software suppliers, whilst language, though still important, is becoming less significant as key multinationals, such as Electrolux or CGS, adopt English as the corporate language. Similarly the move to open systems has meant that national markets are tending to lose their own technical identity and differentiation. On top of this, the ability to operate on a pan-European level is favouring larger players in the field.

The ramifications of this at a macro level within Europe is that individual national markets are becoming more open to foreign competition. As such within national markets, non-domestic companies are becoming increasingly important, whilst key computer service corporations are starting to appear as major market players across the EU. A good illustration of this, evident even over a relatively short space of time, is the decline of indigenous companies in Britain (Table 4.3). A comparison of the top ten largest companies (by revenue) in 1984 and 1991 reveals that British companies have lost their former dominance in the domestic market as major international companies have entered the market through acquisitions. As competition has increased the remaining indigenous British companies have experienced a significant decline in their share of the market. Equally, companies such as CGS, EDS, Andersen Consulting, Sema Group and AT&T Istel (Table 4.4) are establishing a presence in key markets across Europe. Thus EDS has built up a set of key corporate customers, outside its own internal General Motors' demand base (covering Opel, Vauxhall and its stake in Saab Motors) across the main national markets of Europe (Table 4.5). Although this expansion out across Europe by major computer service companies has been supported by often rapid organic growth leading to the establishment of new greenfield operations, in certain European markets it has also been underpinned by merger and acquisition activity. The strategic logic behind this corporate behaviour is two-fold.

First, it has been used to establish a foothold in each of the major European markets, including Britain, Germany, France, Italy and Sweden. Second, major companies are attempting to

Table 4.3 Top ten computer service companies in Britain
(revenue and ownership: 1984 and 1991)

1984	Revenue	Market Share (%)	1991	Revenue	Market Share (%)
1. Thorn EMI (Britain)	57.6	3.8	Sema (France)	412.5	6.5
2. IBM (US)	46.9	3.1	EDS (US)	350.0	5.5
3. Scicon (Britain)	33.4	2.2	P&P (Britain)	228.3	3.6
4. Hoskyns (Britain)	32.3	2.2	Computacenter (Britain)	224.0	3.5
5. Gelsco (US)	29.8	2.0	Hoskyns (France)	200.7	3.2
6. Centre-File (Britain)	29.4	2.0	BT (Britain)	200.0	3.2
7. Logica (Britain)	29.2	2.0	Granada (Britain)	198.8	3.1
8. SD (Britain)	24.6	1.7	Logica (Britain)	197.8	3.1
9. CAP Group (Britain)	23.8	1.6	Dowty (Britain)	192.7	3.0
10. BIS Ltd (Britain)	22.1	1.5	AT&T Istel (US)	185.0	2.9

Source: J. Howells (1987) Developments in the location, technology and industrial organisation of computer services, *Regional Studies* **26**, 493–503. Pierre Audoin Conseil, Namos Ricerca and Richard Holway (1992) *Software and Computing Services Industry in Europe: Volume 1 Markets and Strategies 1992–1996.* PAC/NR/Richard Holway. Paris/London/Milan

add to their portfolio of services to enable them to offer a complete package of services on a pan-European basis. These trends replicate the process during the 1980s, when major domestic companies consolidated their market position through purchasing rival companies. Britain, as in other industrial sectors, has been a particular target for acquisitions by overseas companies with SD-Scicon, Hoskyns, Istel and Sema all being taken over by foreign competitors in the late 1980s and early 1990s.

As a result of these new patterns of competition, organisational change has ensued which has transformed the industry from a set of self-contained national markets to a more integrated European industry. Major computer service firms have employed three organisational strategies to achieve this objective: geographical market segmentation; product market segmentation; and centres of excellence.

First, companies have sought to structure themselves around a number of different country subsidiaries. This is because

Table 4.4 Top 25 software/computing services companies in Europe

Rank	Company	Ownership	European Revenue 1991 (M ecu)
1	IBM	US	2176
2	CGS	F	1271
3	DEC	US	1072
4	EDS	US	887
5	Finsiel	I	836
6	Microsoft	US	825
7	Andersen	US	732
8	Nixdorf	D	633
9	Debis	D	623
10	Sema Group	F	588
11	Computer Ass.	US	467
12	Sligos	F	459
13	Hewlett Packard	US	443
14	Oracle	US	408
15	Olivetti	I	390
16	FTLIS	F	386
17	DATEVeG	D	361
18	SAP	D	344
19	GSI	F	341
20	Thomson CSF	F	322
21	Bull	F	315
22	ICL	JAP	305
23	BT	GB	293
24	Granada	GB	283
25	Logica	GB	282

Source: Pierre Audoin Conseil, Namos Ricerca and Richard Holway (1992) *Software and Computing Services Industry in Europe: Volume 1 Markets and Strategies 1992–1996.* PAC/NR/Richard Holway. Paris/London/Milan

historically each subsidiary has been required to be a separate legal entity. More importantly, it stems from the fact that companies need to provide a good local service. One of the prime reasons for this is language which is of particular importance in the delivery of consultancy or technical services. It has also been associated with a more general trend towards decentralised management practices, flatter organisational structures, allowing greater flexibility and outsourcing to business units and subsidiaries. As a result the major trend in organ-

Table 4.5 Globalisation of computer services: examples of EDS major customers across Europe

Country/Area	Service
Northern Europe	
Heineken (Neth)	Manage IT services
Atlar Copco (Bel)	Systems management
Kredietbank (Bel)	Integration International Banking System
SAAB (Sweden)	Facilities management (FM)
Germany	
Motoren-Mannheim	Systems administration
Ruecker	Systems operation
Opel (General Motors)	FM
Britain	
Midland Bank	Systems management
Dept of Social Security	Operation of computer centres
Vauxhall (General Motors)	FM
France	
France Telecom	Joint venture – to build ISDN applications
Sulzer	Install information management systems
Credit Lyonnais	Operate data centre
Spain	
Renfe	Automatic payment network
Telefonica	Systems management

Source: C. Gentle and J. Howells (1993) *Restructuring for a single market: The computer services industry. Communications and Strategies.* IDATE. France

isational change has been to push down to the lowest level complex market decisions.

Second, the operations of companies have been organised around specific product market sectors. Typically, these sectors include financial services; energy; transportation; telecommunications; and manufacturing. This structure enables rapid response to changes in market demands, allowing the organisational structure to be market driven.

Related to this, 'centres of excellence' have been developed within different country offices taking a lead role in a certain expertise or activity. These centres of excellence draw on the expertise in that office, but also on that country's strength. Typically, for example, financial expertise is centred on London, telecommunications in Paris and manufacturing in Frankfurt or Stuttgart. Companies therefore draw on this local expertise to customise their global service provision.

These corporate dynamics have accelerated the pace of change and created an environment where even the major European players feel they need to increase their market presence. A good example of this is of Cap Gemini Sogeti of France. This company was formed in 1975 from the merger of three companies: Cap (formed in 1962); Sogeti (established in 1967); and Gemini (formed in 1968). In 1986 it purchased IBAT, a German company that specialised in process control and robotics. In the same year it also acquired Gestine Dati, an Italian data processing company which provided services to industry and local government. In 1987, it bought into a US company (Syscomm Systems), a specialist in the financial and telecommunication fields. Data Logic – a Swedish services group with activities in Norway, Denmark and Britain – was its major European acquisition of 1988. During 1989, CGS acquired four more companies to strengthen its domestic position and diversify its international activities. These included two French companies: Apsis and Aptor in Grenoble; Accept Data in Sweden; and Merit Systems in the US. A majority stake in the leading British software house Hoskyns was purchased by CGS in July 1990 (now fully acquired): bringing the further demise of the British services industry. CGS consolidated its position as the leading European company in 1991, with its purchase of Volmac (Netherlands) and Progamator (Sweden). Finally, and potentially the most strategically significant event, was the purchase by CGS of a stake in the software house – Debis Systemhaus – of Daimler-Benz (the German industrial conglomerate). This strategic partnership – which involves Daimler-Benz in turn taking a 34 per cent stake in Sogeti, the holding company of CGS – is a response to the growing competition in the world software market. Although today CGS is somewhat preoccupied by integrating these businesses into a pan-European company. Other such strategic alliances have also been formed, including the agreement between EDS and Compaq allowing EDS to become the world-wide systems integrator for Compaq. In addition, Sema Group is currently negotiating a joint venture with France Telecom, and Logica (Britain) with Finseil (Italy).

What are the implications of this for the industry's structure in Europe? A 'super league' of computer service companies in Europe is now visible. These companies are of sufficient scale to provide a full range of service products across the key national economies of the EU. These companies will open up a gap between themselves and primarily national and sub-national computer service firms who will not have sufficient scale to be able to offer this wider service provision across a set of national markets. By contrast, the bottom end of the industry, in terms of firm size, will still be highly dynamic both in terms of new firm entry and rapid organic growth (often well above 50 per cent per annum) for successful niche companies augmented by judicious acquisitions (such as those undertaken by MicroFocus, Sage and Misys of Britain). However, the recent depressed state of the world economy has meant that new firm formation rates in the industry have undoubtedly dropped and have been accompanied by a high death rate of computer services companies, via insolvency and liquidation.

EUROPEAN RESTRUCTURING FOR THE SINGLE EUROPEAN MARKET

The structure of the European computer services industry is currently undergoing a fundamental change. Evidence gathered from case studies of a number of major players in the industry by the author confirms such a trend. The analysis here seeks to highlight three major shaping factors for tomorrow. These changes are taking place both in patterns of demand within the industry and in new patterns of supply.

CONTRACTING OUT AND EXTERNALISATION

On a more general level, it has already been noted that major industrial corporations are seeking to rationalise and integrate their operations within Europe; to respond more rapidly to the market and technical environment in which they operate[10]. On a more specific level, ongoing developments in the area of contracting out (or outsourcing) and externalisation of products and services continue to be an important factor in the sector's development. These measures have been implemented by companies to improve efficiency, to reduce costs and to become more responsive to changes in patterns of demand. Thus the cost of IT is becoming increasingly expensive for large corporations. This expense is further heightened by the rapid rate of technological obsolescence. At the same time, IT is now a critical part of business planning and is gaining a comparative advantage. Outsourcing – that is the use of third parties to deliver information systems management – includes three aspects:

1. Delivery of information technology (IT) services.
2. Management of assets, such as data centres and networks.
3. The development of a long-term relationship between vendor and corporate customer.

Large corporations have used outsourcing of IT operations to: reduce costs; to increase efficiency; and, to instill greater flexibility in the organisation so it can adjust more rapidly to changing patterns of demand for its products and services.

As the market opportunities increase so do the size and range of services provided by suppliers, in terms of out-sourcing, expand. The range of services offered under the heading 'outsourcing' vary from facilities management and contract programming to high-value added services, such as systems integration. The pressures for outsourcing within large companies remain intense. A survey by IDC[11] suggests that the amount currently spent externally on IT could be only half of the spending internally on IT in terms of internal staffing, training operations, maintenance and IS (Information Systems) planning, thus allowing a potential doubling of the market.

Today, the continued move towards contracting out of com-puter service operations and its influence on the development of the market has been largely due to the process of organisational externalisation and internalisation of major computer service operators by their parent organisation. Some operations have been through a varied ownership history moving from independence into being acquired by a larger non-computer service company and then out again. The history of Data Sciences is an example of this. It originated from two companies, Software Sciences and Datasolve, both established in the 1960s. Datasolve was later purchased by BOC and both these operations were then acquired by Thorn EMI in 1982. In 1991 Data Sciences was created as a management buyout (MBO) of Thorn EMI software, thus returning the company back into an independent operation. Other major computer service operations such as Centrefile (owned by National Westminster Bank) remain firmly embedded in their parent organisation, whilst others, including General Motors' acquisition of EDS in 1984, have moved from independent status to be an operating arm within a major industrial corporation. Indeed, Barclays Bank – the largest British clearing bank – has bid to be a British government facilities management agency[12]: demonstrating how liberalisation has removed traditional divides, especially within services, to facilitate a new dynamic in economic development.

COLLABORATION AND NETWORKING

Although in one sense research and technological development within computer services remains a highly confidential activity, firms involved in the IT sector have increasingly sought to build up strategic alliances[13]. Such software alliances are often between hardware manufacturers and key software suppliers to gain reciprocal access to key sectors and markets, as noted earlier in the case of EDS and Compaq. It has led through to accusations of restrictive practices and monopolistic agreements between leading software producers and the hardware manufacturers that are dependent on key pieces of operating software, such as MSDOS. However, at a purely technical level, such alliances have increased. According to Hagedoorn and Schakenraad[14], computer services recorded the highest growth rates in new technology alliance and joint R&D agreements of all high technology sectors in the late 1980s.

GLOBAL EXPANSION

Some computer service companies have also sought and been able to gain critical mass and global expansion. However, these have been few and far between. What is apparent within the industry is that there are still very few specific computer service companies in a major position within world markets (Table 4.6). They cover CSC, TRW and ADP from the US and Cap Gemini Sogeti of France in terms of computer service operations and a limited number of, mainly US, software companies centred on packaged software including Microsoft, Computer Associates, Oracle and Lotus. However, IT hardware manufacturers (including IBM, Fujitsu, Digital and Siemens), management consultancies (such as Andersen Consulting and Price Waterhouse), telecommunication companies (such as NTT, AT&T and BT), and some major industrial corporations (covering EDS-GM, General Electric and Daimler-Benz), form the bulk of major computer service suppliers. Nevertheless although competition from these other sources will increase, the actual profitability and capital worth of well-run computer service companies can be extremely profitable. Microsoft now has a market capitalisation in excess of IBM whose net worth has been declining; a position which was unthinkable until recently. Indeed the value of these computer service operations within these larger companies may at some stage encourage their unbundling.

SUMMARY

Clearly, the computer services industry in Europe is undergoing a major restructuring. The liberalising of formerly 'closed' member state markets has, together with linguistic, cultural, legal, procurement and close buyer–supplier links, opened up the European market. Indeed, these barriers are becoming less significant over time. Externalisation and contracting out of both computer services activities and businesses, increasing inter-firm collaboration, and for a few, rapid expansion overseas have all been associated with such changes. The shift by hardware manufacturers with their existing international networks into software markets has also

Table 4.6 Global top 15 companies: services and software (1991) ($m)

	Services					Software			
	Revenue $m					Revenue $m			
Company	1991	90	% Change	Market Share	Company	1991	90	% Change	% Market Share
1. EDS (US)	3 666	2 870	27.7	11.3	IBM (US)	10 524	9 952	5.7	31.5
2. Andersen Consulting (US)	2 083	1 670	24.7	16.4	Fujitsu (Jp)	2 513	1 607	56.4	7.5
3. IBM (US)	2 018	1 500	34.5	6.2	Microsoft (US)	2 045	1 323	54.6	6.1
4. CSC (US)	1 944	1 679	15.8	6.0	NEC (Jp)	1 761	1 358	29.7	5.3
5. TRW (US)	1 839	1 739	5.8	5.7	Computer Ass. (US)	1 437	1 311	9.7	4.3
6. ADP (US)	1 810	1 736	4.3	5.6	Oracle (US)	1 085	1 002	8.3	3.2
7. Digital (US)	1 570	1 162	35.1	4.9	Siemens (Gr)	964	926	4.2	2.9
8. Fujitsu (Jp)[1]	1 546	989	56.4	4.8	Hitachi (Jp)	959	798	20.2	2.9
9. Cap Gemini Sogeti (Fr)	1 492	1 465	1.8	4.6	Lotus (US)	829	642	29.1	2.5
10. NTT (Jp)	997	884	12.8	3.1	Digital (US)	796	810	-1.7	2.4
11. American Express (US)	995	827	20.3	3.1	Sema Group (Fr)	641	533	20.1	1.9
12. Price Waterhouse (US)	733	583	25.7	2.3	Novell (US)	633	388	63.0	1.9
13. Nomura (Jp)	706	652	8.3	2.2	Olivetti (It)	631	621	1.5	1.9
14. General Electric (US)	650	600	8.3	2.0	ICL (Jp)	626	492	27.1	1.9
15. PRC (US)	623	632	-1.5	1.9	Finsiel (It)	609	490	24.3	1.8

[1] Fujitsu owns ICL

Source: *Datamation* 15 June 1992

been a major factor in the global spread of the industry. Close physical contacts with customers are still the major factor in the location of the industry. However, with the increasing shift towards PC-based packaged software and the move away from country-based geographical market operational structures, these close physical links are loosening over time and will quicken the formation of the single European market.

Notes

1. There are considerable variations in the definition of computer services; however this chapter will use the definition used by the OECD (1989) which has gained general acceptance and allows comparability between countries. It covers:

   Computer Software: provision of stored programs for computer operating systems for applications, either customised for individual clients or packaged to suit multiple clients. Software may be transmitted to the customer via a telecommunications network, via a transportable medium such as a computer tape, disc or CD-Rom, or as part of a complete hardware and software system (turnkey system).

   Computer Services and Consultancy: provision of services from supplier to customer which may involve the supplier carrying out data processing activities using the supplier's own facilities (bureaux services), or using a customer's facilities (facilities management). Alternatively the supplier may assist the customer to carry out his own data processing by helping with systems design (systems analysis and consultancy) by providing staff to work on the customer's site ("bodyshopping"), or by providing training and education services.

   The OECD also includes computerised information services in its definition of computer-based services.

   See: OECD (1985) *Software: An Emerging Industry ICCP Report 9.* Organisation for Economic Co-operation and Development. Paris. OECD (1989) *Working Party on Telecommunication and Information Services Policy.* Organisation for Economic Co-operation and Development. Paris (DSTI/ICCP/TISP/88.9), 18pp. Also J. Howells (1989) *Trade in Software, Computer Services and Computerised Information Services.* Report to the Directorate for Science, Technology and Industry, Organisation for Economic Co-operation and Development. Paris (DST/ICCP/TISP/89.16), 172 pp.

2. Peat Marwick McLintock (1988) *The Cost of Non-Europe for Business Services.* CEC. Luxembourg. P. 19. See also A. Knight and D. Silk (1990) *Managing Information.* McGraw Hill. London.

3. CEC (1991) *Panorama of EC Industries, 1991–1992.* CEC. Luxembourg, pp. 16–29.

4. Pierre Audoin Conseil, Namos Ricerca and Richard Holway (1992) *Software and Computing Services Industry in Europe: Volume 1 Markets and*

Strategies 1992–1996. PAC/NR/Richard Holway. Paris/London/Milan.

5. R. Miles (1993) Outsider takes over at the helm at IBM. *Computing.* 1 April 1993.

6. Pierre Audoin Conseil, Namos Ricerca and Richard Holway (1992) *Software and Computing Services Industry in Europe: Volume 1 Markets and Strategies 1992–1996.* PAC/NR/Richard Holway. Paris/London/Milan.

7. M. A. Cusumano (1991) *Japan's Software Factories: A Challenge to US Management.* Oxford University Press. New York. See also *The Economist* (1993) Japan's software wars. 25 September 1994.

8. D. Martin (1992) Bull chases Britain deals in India. *Computing.* 3 April 1992.

9. Andersen Consulting (1992) *Trends in Information Technology.* Sunday Times/McGraw Hill. London. M. R. Irwin and M. Merenda (1987) The network as corporate strategy *Transnational Data and Communications Report* **10**, 17–20.

10. Yankee Group Europe (1991) 'Outsourcing in Europe', The Yankee Group Europe, Watford, 11.3, pp. 1–14. See also J. Howells (1989b) Externalisation and the formation of new industrial operations *Area 21,* 289–299.

11. International Data Corporation (1992). London.

12. R. Preston (1993) Barclays on short list to buy DoT computer services agency *Financial Times* 14 June 1993 p. 1.

13. W. Dawkins (1992) The network links up *Financial Times* 25 November 1992, p. 16.

14. J. Hagedoorn and J. Schakenraad (1991) 'The Role of Inter-Firm Co-operation Agreements in the Globalisation of Economy and Technology', Fast Occasional Paper 280, DGXII, CEC. Brussels, p. 95.

5 European Telecommunications

INTRODUCTION

The telecommunications industry provides what is the classic example of the dilemma facing European industries in an era after liberalisation. Today we stand at the dawn of the 'information age'. For some time now it has been predicted that information will be all powerful in determining the competitiveness of modern industrial economies. At the heart of this new information age are telecommunication services. Telecommunication networks provide the arteries along which information – the lifeblood of the information age – can flow. The speed of technological change is denoted by the pulse of information along these information highways, or Infobahns as they have become known in Eurospeak.

In contrast to this bright new future is the reality facing Europe. In particular, the nub of the problem is about how to aid and support the transition of the telecommunications industry from a set of fragmented markets to a unified market which is globally competitive. It is imperative that this mutation takes place not only because it is expected that telecommunications will be the fastest growth sector in the rest of the 1990s, but that the telecommunications industry is central to the overall global competitiveness of the European economy. Liberalisation has been the principal instrument that has been used to bring about this transition.

Prior to the 1980s European telecommunication companies were characterised by the state monopolies, which often also controlled postal services. These PTTs – postal, telegraph and telecommunication organisations – dominated telecommunication services with few if any exceptions. In turn, these national service monopolies supported national transmission equipment manufacturers. For instance, in Germany Deutsche Bundespost Telekom was supplied with telephone switching systems by Siemens; likewise in Holland, Netherlands PTT was supplied by Phillips. These relationships created nationally based telecommunication services and networks, with little, if any, competition. As a result, investment was slow to flow into new technology. The service consisted of a basic telephony connection, with few customer orientated options. Consequently, Europe entered the 1990s with a telecommunications industry that was both technologically backward and globally uncompetitive.

It is against this background that this chapter is set. There are three major themes that are beginning to emerge and that will dominate the pace of development of the European telecommunications industry well into the next century. These are: the speed and direction of liberalisation; corporate responses to liberalisation; and third, the convergence of technology which is the driving force underlying many of the developments associated with the telecommunications industry. These three themes provide the main threads of the discussion in this chapter, as the past developments and future trends are weaved together to illuminate the coming pattern of what promises to be one of Europe's most important industries. But exactly how important will the telecommunications industry be to the European economy? It is to this question that we turn first.

THE SIZE AND ECONOMIC IMPORTANCE OF TELECOMMUNICATIONS

Telecommunications is one of the most important industries in the European economy, both in its direct and indirect contribution. Indeed, in 1992 just under one million people were employed directly in state-owned (or formerly state-owned) European telecommunication companies (Table 5.1). In addition, there are many thousands of other jobs in mobile communications, and new companies that have entered into telecommunications markets. Indirectly, telecommunications supports countless other jobs in related areas, including telecommunications equipment manufacturing, software services and a host of other industries which are converging with telecommunications.

In terms of the size of the EU telecoms market it is dominated by four countries: Germany, Britain, France and Italy (Table 5.2). Together these four countries account for

After Liberalisation

Table 5.1   Employment in European
telecommunications 1991–2

Company	Employment
OTE (Greece	27 632
PTT (Netherlands)	30 638
Telecom Italia (Italy)	89 575
Telefonica (Spain)	75 568
TeleDanmark (Denmark)	17 903
Telecom Eireann (Ireland)	13 514
Telecom Portugal (Portugal)	17 000
British Telecom (Britain)	209 836
Belgacom (Belgium)	27 702
Deutsche Telekom (Germany)	228 571
France Telecom (France)	157 754
Total	895 693

Source: Author's calculations

over four-fifths of the market for telephony services in Europe. There are two important consequences of this distribution of the market across the EU. First, as liberalisation takes effect in the rest of the 1990s, it will be these four countries that will drive the dynamics of change: largely because they have inherited the largest monopoly power.

The other point to note is that many of the smaller markets will be important because it is through these countries that new entrants are likely to establish a foothold in the European market, since privatisation offers up such opportunities to build a market base. One separate and final point on the structure of the market in Europe is the overwhelming importance of domestic calls, which are estimated to account for around 90 per cent of the market. The rest of the market is divided between 7 per cent international calls outside the EU and 3 per cent intra EU calls.

The industry is also one of the most dynamic sectors in the European economy. In addition, the potential for growth is significant. Witness the example of the US. The US economy is roughly twice the size of the Japanese and four times that of the European economy; the number of calls made is higher than

Table 5.2   The European telecommunications market

Country	Total revenue 1990 Ecu m	%
Germany	21 227	23.7
Britain	18 671	20.8
France	17 988	20.1
Italy	14 537	16.2
Spain	6 225	6.9
Netherlands	4 193	4.7
Belgium	2 371	2.6
Denmark	2 113	2.3
Ireland	987	1.1
Portugal	970	1.1
Greece	153	0.1
Luxembourg	153	0.1
EU	89 588	100

Source: European Commission

in Japan by a factor of seven and higher than in Europe by a factor of fifteen. This example goes some way to illustrate the potential for growth in Europe, although the traffic intensity of the US is partly a function of the geography of that economy.

However, what is far more significant is that the telecommunications industry is of greater importance to the EU economy than the contribution in pure economic terms. The telecommunications industry is a key component in the future of the European economy in terms of growth, competitiveness and employment.

As modern industrial economies become increasingly mature and complex, the need for knowledge grows apace. Here parallels with the mushrooming of the world economy can be drawn. Globalisation of the economic activity has seen the international expansion and integration of key corporate functions such as production, marketing, and research and development. More importantly, it has heralded new ways of transforming knowledge via technology into goods and services.

Nowhere has this growth been greater than in the international financial markets. The liberalisation of financial markets – detailed in Chapter 3 – has led to the development of capital markets based around twenty-four hour trading. Within this global system a 'book', such as a portfolio of foreign exchange trading, is typically passed in turn continuously from New York, to London, through to Tokyo, and back to New York for the next day's trading. It is only via telecommunication networks that financial markets have been able to blossom. The volume of growth expected in transatlantic traffic – the bulk of which is financial traffic – can be gauged by the ordering in 1993 of a new fibre optic cable to link the US and the EU. Called Tat-12, it has about five times the capacity of the last system, and a phenomenal twelve times the call volume of the first system built in the mid-1980s.

Within financial centres, telecommunications have altered the structure of markets. Prior to liberalisation, many financial markets were based around physical trading, take for instance the London equities market. Post 'Big Bang', however, trading is now screen based, but is dependent on value-added information networks; although this is not to argue that close physical and social contact is also essential in the functioning of financial markets. Overall, the quality and technological sophistication of telecommunication services plays a critical role in the relative competitiveness of financial markets. Indeed, it could be argued that this is one reason why London retains its pre-eminence as Europe's leading financial centre over rivals such as Frankfurt and Paris.

The rapid growth in areas such as global finances has led to the massive cumulative rise in international traffic. In 1992, it is estimated that the market for international telecommunications traffic grew by approximately 13 per cent. This was some ten times the growth in EU GDP during the same year. Projections of the likely growth in international traffic expect to see an almost exponential rate in coming years. Similar measures of growth show that telecommunications has consistently outperformed economic growth in most regions of the global economy.

Will growth in telecommunications continue? It is estimated that the telecommunications industry accounts for an annual market in terms of services of Ecu 285 bn at a global level and

Ecu 84 bn in the EU. In addition, the equipment market is estimated to be worth Ecu 82 bn at the global level and Ecu 26 bn in the EU[1]. A projection made on behalf of the EC forecast that the sector will have one of the most dynamic growth rates throughout the rest of this decade – services growing by eight per cent and four per cent for equipment each year until the year 2000. At this point in time it is forecast that the telecommunications sector will account for six per cent of GDP, not including the indirect effects on the economy as a whole of network installation and operation. This growth will be (further) fuelled by the liberalisation and privatisation of telecommunication services in the EU.

THE HISTORY OF EU TELECOMMUNICATIONS LIBERALISATION 1984-98

Prior to the 1980s, the regulation of telephony services in Europe was based purely on national controls. Indeed, in many countries the PTT organisations were in effect government departments. The EC played little if any role. Transnational regulation was in place via the International Telegraphy Union (ITU), which was founded in 1865 by several European telegraph administrations. It has been the ITU, and its associated bodies, that have controlled the global development of telecommunications.

Indeed, the majority of ITU members in the 1980s were very much opposed to liberalisation. In this context, PTTs in Europe were no different. In fact, many of Europe's telecoms companies were at the forefront in maintaining state monopolies. However, Japan, USA and Britain broke away from the monopoly mentality of the ITU. It was this schism in the ITU which drove the liberalisation that was to sweep through Europe in the 1990s. Underpinning this shift was the rise of the free-market Thatcher and Reagan administrations.

It was against this background that the EC first entered the fray. In 1983, it decided that it would develop policies on high-technology and information industries. The EC concluded that the 'nationally protected environment that fragmented European telecommunications was an important factor in Europe's weak competitive position relative to the USA and Japan'[2].

Table 5.3   Major landmarks in the liberalisation of EU
telecommunications

Date	Landmark
Nov. 1984	Implementation of harmonisation in the field of telecommunications (84/549/EEC).
Nov. 1984	First phase of opening up access to public telecommunications terminal equipment.
Dec. 1986	Decision to standardisation in information technology and telecommunications.
Jun. 1987	Green Paper on the development of the Common Market for Telecommunication Services and Equipment (Com (87) 290).
Apr. 1988	Formation of ETSI
May 1988	Commission Directive on competition in the markets in telecommunications terminal equipment ((88/301/EEC).
Jun. 1989	Adoption of framework relating to open network provision (90/387/EEC).
Jun. 1990	Commission Directive on competition in the market for telecommunication services (90/338/EEC).
Nov. 1990	Green Paper on a common approach to satellite communications in the EC (Com (90) 490).
Jun. 1991	Guidelines on the application of EEC competition rules in the telecommunications sector (91/C233/02).
Oct. 1992	1992 review of the situation in telecommunications services sector (Sec (92) 1048).
Jun. 1993	Council resolution on the liberalisation of telecommunications services in EU by 1998.

Source: Various CEC

Since the EC first attempted to liberalise the telecommunications industry in the early 1980s, there have been three
distinct stages: the complex chronology that lies behind this
history is outlined in Table 5.3. The first stage came about in
late 1984 with the adoption of the first action programme in
the telecommunications sector. The second began in 1987 with
the release of the EC's Green Paper on telecommunications
services and equipment, which was formally endorsed in 1988[3].
It was during this stage that the EC first began to evolve a
cohort view of the development of the industry on a pan-
European basis. The final stage began in 1992 with the

publication of the Commission's report *Review of the situation in the telecommunications services sector*[4]. It was on the basis of this report that the Council of Telecommunication Ministers adopted the historic resolution to liberalise European telecommunications.

In the first stage, the initial objective of the EC was to coordinate the future development of telecommunications, in particular in areas such as ISDN (Integrated Services Digital Network), Digital Mobile Communications, the introduction of broadband communications, the establishment of common standards for harmonisation, and to support pre-competitive research and development. The identification of telecommunications as key to the future competitiveness of the European economy marked a rapid expansion for support of the sector. A number of initiatives were developed to implement EC policy, such as the RACE (research and development in integrated broadband communications), STAR (development of telecommunications in peripheral regions), and measures to promote European standards as global standards to give Europe a lead in new technologies and markets such as GSM (global system for mobile communications). In particular, this policy was formalised via the formation of ETSI (European Telecommunications Standards Institute) based in France in 1988.

Arguably of greater importance to the future of the PTTs was the extension of EC powers with the publication of the Green Paper adopted in June 1988, to cover regulatory matters and open up the sector to competition: marking the start of a new era in the European telecommunications industry. There were three drivers of change that brought about the Green Paper[5]:

- the fragmentation of the European market for telecommunication networks and services and its increasing importance for the EU, from a macro-economic perspective;
- the inadequacy of existing regulatory arrangements, based around member state regulation and, the antiquated nature of these systems meant that the EU was not in a position to deal with the rapid developments in new technologies and markets;
- a wave of global liberalisation which began in the US with

the dismantling of the AT&T monopoly, and the splitting of domestic and international services in Japan.

It was against this background that it was decided that Europe needed to develop a single, co-ordinated telecommunications policy, so as to ensure that the industry would not be left behind its direct competitors.

The guiding principles adopted by the EU to ensure this transition from state monopolies to an open and competitive telecommunications environment was based on six elements. First, the full liberalisation of the equipment market and the establishment of common standards for mutual recognition between manufacturers to maximise the synergies across the single market. The second involved the separation of regulatory and operational functions within Member States. This element was critical to the foundations of liberalisation across the EU, for one of the main pillars supporting the monopoly situation existing in most countries was the control of services either by a state corporation or a government department. The third element was the harmonising of telecommunication services across the EU. The main basis for achieving this was the notion of ONP (open network provision). However, this notion has proved far from easy to adopt since it is based on opening up telecommunication infrastructures to all carriers. Competition law was also co-opted to ensure that discriminatory practices and the abuse of dominant positions by operators and service providers did not take place: this has been the fourth element. Fifth, the EC brought the industry in line with the common policies being adopted by the Uruguay Round of GATT. Finally, and most importantly, the progressive and ultimate liberalisation of the market for telecommunications services was enacted.

This historic moment in European telecommunications history came on 16 June 1993, at a meeting of the EU, Member States adopted a resolution to liberalise all public telephony services by 1998. The Cohesion Four of Spain, Portugal, Ireland and Greece were granted until 2003 in which to prepare their telecommunication systems for open competition. The background to the adoption of this historic move was, in part, driven by the number of bottlenecks highlighted in the 1992 review. One of the major problems identified was the high cross-border tariffs throughout the EU, which showed little relation to geography. The large differentials that exist between the price of calls between member states shows that if a call is made from Lisbon to Madrid the cost per unit call under current regimes is Ecu 2.72. In contrast, the reverse call from Madrid to Lisbon costs an extra Ecu 0.3. Whilst a caller from Denmark to Germany will be charged the same tariff as calling Greece, in spite of the fact that there could be several thousand miles difference in the destination of the call.

The main economic consequences of the decision to liberalise EU telecommunications are fourfold. First, to involve nearly 85 per cent of operators' income of a market totalling around Ecu 100 billion. Second, to bring substantial changes to the conditions and means of safeguarding universal service, in particular to ensure the social and economic cohesion of the disadvantaged regions. Third, to give a stimulus to the economy and the market in generating investment in technology, research and services. Finally, to radically alter the structure of the industry from one dominated by state monopoly PTTs to competitive markets involving the provision of telephony and value-added services by a host of domestic and international companies. But also to foster competition between fixed telephony services and competing technologies such as mobile and value-added services.

The challenges facing Europe after liberalisation are significant indeed. Not least for the Cohesion Four who arguably have the least developed telecommunications infrastructures. Hence, the extension granted to these countries further compounds this problem, in that it offers the opportunity to further delay the required costly investment. However, in the intervening period since the announcement of liberalisation there has been little evidence to suggest that these countries will sit back and allow the more advanced areas of the EU to increase the significant gap that already exists in the technological capabilities of their telecommunication networks. The solution sought has been to attract foreign telecommunication giants to take a stake in the state operators, so as to shoulder some of the heavy investment burden. For instance, in the recent past the policy of OTE in Greece of pursuing a piecemeal replacement of switching and transmission was further fragmenting the telecommunications network. In 1994 there were more than 800 000 applicants for telephone lines outstanding. Indeed, the Greek authorities estimate that the network requires Ecu 5 bn over the next decade. It is against this backdrop that OTE is now to be privatised.

A second and common problem is that because of the different situation of each PTT, the pace and direction of liberalisation will be very different across the EU. Telecommunications across the EU are very different and this will cause major problems during liberalisation. A flavour of the level of service and the idiosyncrasies of each member state is presented below to illustrate the qualitative gaps that exist across the EU (Box 5.1).

Box 5.1: European Telecommunications

- Belgium: Telecommunication services are generally above the average level in Europe. Prices for both local and mobile services are less than the average across the EU, although slightly higher for international services and leased lines. ISDN is now available and the Belgium government is now broaching the issue of liberalising the industry.

- Denmark: Much of the network is already digitised which has resulted from the relatively liberal regime in operation. There are four regional companies, which provide one of the best services in the EU. Local international and mobile tariffs are some of the lowest in the EU.

- France: France Telecom has created possibly the best telecommunications network in the EU. Indeed, the fact that it has been established in a monopoly system, with no competition, has been one of the primary points of contention against the liberalisation of European telecommunications services. It is estimated that digitisation covers over 90 per cent of customers. ISDN has been available in a number of cities since 1988, including Paris and Marseilles. International calls are below the EU average, but tariffs on mobile phones are prohibitive.

- Germany: The first step in the liberalisation of Deutsche Telekom came with the separation of equipment provision from other services. However, there are a number of problems for the network and improving its efficiency. All employees have civil service status, hence Germany has the highest number of employees in Europe, indeed nearly a quarter of all jobs are in Germany. Also with the reunification a great deal of investment is required to upgrade eastern Federal Districts. This has resulted in the digitisation of the network, which will reduce the number of local exchanges from 500 to just 90. The tariff structure still remains the highest in the EU.

- Greece: After much political wrangling OTE – the state-owned telecommunications operator – is to be privatised. However, it will be some time before private capital will overcome the years of under-investment in the network. In particular, the network is only just starting to digitise the network and to introduce ISDN.

- Ireland: Eireann Telecom has made major steps in improving the quality of services, although national charges are still expensive. Many of these changes have been driven by the desire to attract inward investors into the country. Recently, a tranche of the state-owned corporation was sold to Cable and Wireless, the international telecommunications giant, as a first step towards privatisation.

- Italy: The Italian telecommunications network has been undergoing some of the most radical changes in the EU. Once characterised by bureaucracy, poor services and complex concessionary companies, the major change has been driven by forging together the former companies, SIP and STET, into a single telecommunications company: Telecom Italia. In general, much investment is still required to upgrade the standard of services, in particular in the deprived southern Mezzogiorno.

- The Netherlands: Considered as one of the best telecommunication services in the EU. KPN – the state-owned company – privatisation will result in a golden share still being held by the government. Since the late 1980s, there has been a substantial increase in telephone lines and local, national and international call volumes. The network and the markets it commands are, however, small in comparison to other Euro-telecoms giants such as France Telecom.

- Portugal: Portugal's telecommunications networks suffer from many of the problems experienced by the 'poorer' Cohesion Four members of the EU. Charges are high for both national and international calls. In addition, there are high fault rates and long waiting times. However, the system is being quickly up-graded, in particular with monies from Brussels under programmes such as STAR, improving digitisation for inward investors.

- Spain: Since the mid-1980s, the telecoms market has been undergoing dramatic changes, in part resulting from an explosion in demand. A new deal has been struck between the regulatory and Telefonica provisions have been made to liberalise progressively the market for services. The so-called Telecommunications Plan establishes the grounds for an ambitious investment programme, to be financed by a radical overhaul of the tariff structure.

- UK: In 1983 British Telecom (BT) set in motion the liberalisation of the industry in Europe. The opening up of the industry was a controlled process with only one operator – Mercury Communications (the British subsidiary of Cable and Wireless) – licensed to compete in fixed link telephony services to private and business customers. This process also involved the separation of the operators (BT and Mercury) from the regulatory body: OFTEL. A study by the British government has ranked British telecommunications 'a good second' internationally to the US. Nonetheless, although competition has brought much capital investment into the network, Britain still has some of the highest – but quickest falling – tariffs in Europe. In 1993, Britain took liberalisation a step further by granting licences to other operators including AT&T, Energis, Iconica and City Telecommunications.

As the countries of the EU adopt the liberalisation directive, each will move at its own speed and initially in its own direction. The effect of this combination of forces mean that it will be some time before the liberalisation process generates any significant momentum. The process has to face what appear to be the near intractable situations such as the civil servant status of all PTT staff in Germany.

The picture of how the European telecommunications industry will develop into the next century, however, is more complex than the mere speed at which the EC achieves the liberalisation. Another dimension needs to be added in order to comprehend how the forces of liberalisation are being shaped by technological change. More precisely, we are moving into an age of mobile communications, which will grab a growing tranche of the former monopoly market held by PTTs for communication for both voice and data, due to the encroaching wireless revolution.

A WIRELESS REVOLUTION: TELECOMMUNICATIONS AND NEW TECHNOLOGY

The speed by which the liberalisation of telecommunications suddenly rose to the top of the European political agenda in the early 1990s was largely a consequence of the emerging information revolution. Indeed, we are already in the midst of this dramatic transition, reflected most graphically by the cyberspace and virtual reality opportunities offered up by multi-media services delivered directly into the home.

Aside from these possibilities, the growth of traditional telephony services, and the technological infrastructure that underpins them, is a very real threat to the PTTs. The revenues of European PTTs will be squeezed from three directions in the future: network developments in the local loop; long-distance competition; and – what is termed here as – wireless and mobile communication technologies (WMC).

LOCAL LOOP TELEPHONY: THE KEY TO DELIVERING MULTI-MEDIA SERVICES INTO THE HOME

For many years the possibility of information services delivered into the home for the consumption of armchair recipients has been touted. Against this futuristic vision was the reality that the local infrastructure, – termed the local loop – the telecoms network that connects together the home in a neighbourhood to the local switch into the national network, did not have the capacity to deliver such services into the home in much of the EU.

However, it is possible to envisage in the future that the infrastructure will be upgraded. Indeed, many of the trunk networks across the EU have already been digitised, particularly in France where a large proportion of the network has been upgraded to ISDN. Also, many local areas across Europe will see the development of cable networks to facilitate the delivery of multi-media services. To examine the way in which PTTs may face competition in the local loop from cable operators in future, it is instructive to study a country at the forefront in this process – Britain.

It is estimated that some Ecu 30 billion will be invested in Britain in cable networks over the last six years of this century[6]. The advanced state of the British cable network is indicated by the fact that some Baby Bells – US regional telephony companies – believe that their British joint ventures will be further advanced in developing the information highway than their US sister companies.

In the 1980s, British policy was primarily based on the reasoning that the development of cable could be financed purely through entertainment-led services. However, it has become increasingly evident over the last decade that cable on its own did not provide the basis for a viable business. As a result few of the 127 franchises that had been granted were operational.

As Cornford and Gillespie[7] rightly note:

> *although television services are obviously important to cable operations, increasingly in the 1990s the force driving the cable companies to build networks is the opportunity to offer telephony....*

*by January 1993 50 of the 58 operating broadband franchises were
already or planning to introduce it before the end of that year.*

The 1991 Duopoly Review encouraged the cable operators –
a total of 27 companies, 20 of them North American, have the
127 franchises between them – to provide telephony services in
the light of the decision by the other major competitor
Mercury in the duopoly to BT, to cherry pick in the long-
distance market, rather than battle it out in the local market.
Cable operators have been further aided by the ruling that bars
BT from offering cable television services. Consequently, it will
be cable telephony services that will be a major driving force of
competition in the local loop market.

The other European PTTs will also have to face increasing
competition in the local loop. Already there are major utilities
in both France and Germany gearing up to provide telephony
services, and in some cases a raft of multimedia services, in
local markets. In France, for instance, the water company
Compagnie Generale des Eaux, has established a radio
transmission system in Paris to compete for local calls. While in
Germany, energy giant Veba has in place fibre optic links to
nearly half a million homes, by which it will provide telephony
services, and via a joint venture future multi-media services.

LONG-DISTANCE COMPETITION

There is evidence to suggest that Europe could possibly leap-
frog the US in the race to create a state-of-the-art information
highway. In spite of the fact that Europe has lagged in this race
for some time, the delayed decision to liberalise telecommunications may be a cloud with a silver lining. In that it will
enable the rapid transition from the monopolistic long-
distance and local loop networks, to a plethora of private and
competing networks. A significant shift in this direction came
in spring of 1994 when a consortium of 30 European based
manufacturing companies selected BT and a group led by
AT&T to build competing private networks that will by-pass
local telephone companies with more sophisticated services:

thus effectively cracking open the EU market for telephony services before the official deadline of 1998.

In addition to these changes in the market for corporate telephony business, the monopoly of PTTs for residential customers is under attack. What we are seeing is the development of competing carriers. Again this process is most heavily advanced in Britain. Long-distance carriers have been slow to enter the residential market due to the method of liberalisation employed in Britain, after the privatisation of BT. Until the start of the 1990s the regulator permitted only a duopoly situation in which Mercury competed head-to-head. Mercury throughout this time made little impression on the BT monopoly, so that by 1994 BT still had 85 per cent of the British market[8].

However, in Britain the market has now been opened up to a number of operators including AT&T from the US. In the early 1990s, BT's share of the residential market was falling at a rate of three per cent per year, but with extra competition its monopoly position could now be well and truly broken. In addition, the cable companies have now formed regional networks so that subscribers to telephony services will have the option to call long-distance via this network. Also, other competition will come from a range of companies and technologies, such as Iconica which offers radio transmission calls, British Rail Telecom using its track-side fibre optic network, and Energis which has built a network along the national electricity grid. Across the rest of Europe, it is likely that similar forms of competition will follow a similar path to that in Britain, after the privatisation of the PTT. However, the most significant challenge to PTTs in a period after liberalisation will come from wireless technologies.

WIRELESS AND MOBILE TELECOMMUNICATIONS

A decade ago it would have been almost unthinkable that mobile telecommunications would pose any threat to fixed telephony services provided by PTTs. Today, the greatest challenge to PTT revenues comes from the growth of WMC. It is forecast by the EC that the pace of growth in mobiles will increase and its share of the market will grow from 2.5 per cent

Table 5.4   Biggest US takeover deals

Bidder	Target	Value ($)	Year
1. KKR	RJR Nabisco	24.6 bn	1988
2. Beecham	SmithKline	16.1 bn	1989
3. Chevron	Gulf	13.2 bn	1984
4. Philip Morris	Kraft	13.1 bn	1988
5. AT&T	McCaw Cellular	12.3 bn	1993
6. Bristol-Myers	Squibb	12.0 bn	1989
7. Time	Warner	11.7 bn	1989
8. Texaco	Getty Oil	10.1 bn	1984
9. Du Pont	Conoco	8.0 bn	1981
10. BP	Standard Oil	7.8 bn	1987

Source: *Financial Times* 17 August 1993

to 13 per cent of total telecommunication revenues by the year 2000.

The rise of mobile telecommunications has been a global phenomenon. In the early 1980s mobile telephones were virtually unknown. The rapid growth has not been spread evenly, with Japan and the rest of the world showing only modest growth compared with the US and Europe. In these two regions, there has been near exponential growth: there were some 15m subscribers in the US by 1993.

It is this rate of growth that led to one of the largest take-overs in corporate history (Table 5.4). AT&T paid over $12 billion for McCaw Cellular Communications in 1993; illustrating the potential challenge that WMC can make to the fixed telephony and other voice and data services. The emergence of what might be called the 'wireless revolution' is shown in Figure 5.1. Again we can see the commercial logic of major players seeking to buy into this revolution. Growth is anticipated in both consumer and business markets, with perhaps hundreds of millions of users, in a growing and diverse set of applications.

Indeed, many see analogies between the rise of wireless communications and the technological redundancy of other infrastructure links. For instance, early railways provided local connections to canals. In turn, the first cars in the US were used by farmers to ferry goods to rail links. Today, the

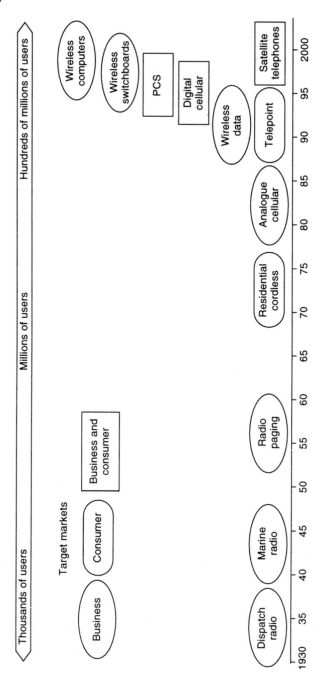

Figure 5.1   The wireless revolution
Source: Motorola

technology is now at hand to provide a serious challenge to the fixed wire carriers for the first time. In particular, the emergence of digital capabilities has increased capacity and quality. Also, mobility is growing most notably through digital assistants – personal mobile offices – which allow an array of computing and data transmission services. These are being further developed by the advances in compressing the electro-magnetic spectrum to send more information.

However, we must not get too carried away with the potential of wireless and mobile communications. The reality is that wireless communications are likely to complement, rather than replace fixed technologies over the next decade. Fixed wire has two distinct key advantages. First, it is still far cheaper than wireless technologies. It will be some time before there is comparable competition. Second, what fixed services lose in mobility they gain in the capacity of their networks. What we can expect to see in the future are complementary and interdependent networks, with global players such as AT&T providing a range of voice and data transmission services by both wireless and fixed technologies. In particular it is important for major players to have mobile phones in the portfolio of services, since they can provide businesses and consumers single billing arrangements, personal numbering and attractive 'one-stop' packages.

Simplistic notions of wireless communications sweeping away fixed line telephony should be quickly discarded. This is not to deny that WMC will be of increasing importance. The possi-bilities are genuinely exciting. Take, for instance, Motorola's ambitious Iridium project. It plans to spend $4 billion to ring the earth with 66 low-earth-orbit (LEO) satellites that will create a mobile 'network' that will enable calls from anywhere on earth. Undoubtedly these developments pose a serious threat to the revenues of European PTTs. As noted earlier in this chapter, the GSM standard is being adopted around the globe as the standard technical platform. This will be of future advantage to European PTTs, at least those that have taken a stake in new and dynamic mobile companies.

It is to this battle which we now turn. The old state PTTs, as we have seen, face stiff competition from all directions that is and will increasingly eat away at their revenues. As liberalis-ation takes effect it will force the PTTs to develop strategies that meet this complex and diverse challenge that encompasses competition from every direction: cable television operators, mobile communications, and multi-national data services.

CORPORATE ALLIANCES AND THE EMERGING GLOBAL TELECOMS MARKET

The actual movers and shakers that will play out the market consequences of liberalisation will be the major telecommunication companies, such as France Telecom and Deutsche Telekom, released from the chains of state monopoly. The emergence of global telecoms carriers is now clearly definable on the horizon, but what will be the forces of change and corporate strategies which will be employed post-liberalisation?

The major market for telecommunication services is for residential customers. This is without doubt the most important market for any incoming company to capture. However, to quote a report by McKinsey[9] comparing different global industries earlier in the 1990s:

> *Even after the wave of deregulation and privatisation in the 1980s, the telecommunications industry remains one of the most heavily regulated industries.*

Therefore, in the future although the walls of regulation have been breached, it will be some time before there is an open and competitive market for voice telephony services throughout Europe. The example of Britain is instructive here. The privatisation of BT in 1984 and the establishment of a duopoly resulted in only limited decline in revenues for the former state-owned utility. Indeed, it has taken a full decade and the licensing of other carriers to bring about any semblance of competition in the British market. The process across the rest of Europe will not necessarily be as slow, since privatisations are planned before the 1998 European Commission deadline. More importantly, competition will flood in via the liberal markets of Britain.

Within this environment the PTTs will have to adopt new strategies to make the transition from state-controlled, utility-orientated to market-driven international telecommunication companies. This is a an extremely difficult transformation to undergo, since it involves a complete change in the culture of the organisation, the purpose of the company from public service to profit, and level of technology employed. These are very real challenges and demand changes in the productivity of the organisation. For it will be the level of productivity achieved by companies that will be the key differentiating factor beyond the millennium.

The most in-depth and authoritative perspective of such differences in global service industries is a study by management consultants McKinsey[10]. The principal finding of this study was that in the telecommunications industry the differences in productivity between the major carriers across the board is due to differences in the organisation of labour within each company. It is instructive to examine some of the key findings of this report. To illustrate the point France Telecom operates a network comparable to that of BT, but with 40–50 000 fewer staff. It is likely that BT will continue to pursue its savage rate of staff cuts for the foreseeable future, in order to improve productivity and hence, competitiveness.

For any carrier hoping to be a successful competitor in the global telecommunications market of the twenty-first century economies of scale will be crucial. It is possible to identify four components that will contribute to the effects of scale:

- network scale, in terms of the number of lines;
- network growth, as too fast growth can lead to diseconomies of scale and reduced labour productivity;
- network density, providing services to a higher density of population aids productivity;
- network topography; the composition of the network.

The ratio between the number of phones and the number of calls will not generate extra business. Evidence from the US shows that over the last 50 years there has been virtually no change in this ratio. Hence, it is of even greater importance for companies to improve productivity to improve competitiveness. Indeed, other evidence from the US suggests that it is only long distance calls that have any degree of elasticity. It is in this market then that the greatest degree of competition can be expected, rather than in the local markets. This process is already taking shape in the market for services, especially to carry data for multi-national companies.

Perhaps the most significant move towards a pan-European market for telecommunications has come with the formation of corporate alliances to serve the needs of multi-national companies. In 1993 and 1994 two deals transformed the international telecommunications landscape. First, BT pledged to take a stake in MCI, the third largest carriers in the US. The deal, worth $4.3 billion, plus a further $750 million to create a joint venture company – Concert – will provide global integrated network services to international companies. The second multi-billion dollar link-up, and potentially the most significant, was between France Telecom and Deutsche Telekom, purchasing a $4.2 billion 20 per cent stake in Sprint, the second largest US carrier. The three companies have established a joint venture to supply to the same market as Concert. This alliance builds on the forging of a close alliance between the French and German carriers.

Add to these corporate power plays the might of AT&T which has yet to wed a partner, but has significant global power; and Cable and Wireless, the most international of telecommunication companies with interests in Britain and Europe, the Far East, in particular Hong Kong and other key global markets. In addition, Unisource formed from collaboration between Swedish, Dutch and Swiss PTTs and Japan's international carriers KDD, illustrates the degree of competition in the international market.

Indeed, it is now possible to define an international telecommunications industry. Ranking the top ten international carriers, Europe accounts for six out of the ten (Table 5.5). However, the Euro big three of Deutsche Telekom, France Telecom and BT are significantly smaller than AT&T. Although it is important to note that the rate of growth is expanding rapidly especially in Germany. We can expect to see greater growth in the future with deeper call penetration between EU countries. In addition growth should result from the progressive opening up of revenues of the former PTTs to competition (Table 5.6). By 1997 the market for telecommunications services should be at least partially developed, with all European companies having a third of their revenues exposed to competitive pressures.

Table 5.5　Top ten international telecommunication carriers

		MITT[1] (m) 1992
1. AT&T	US	6 984
2. Deutsche Telekom	Germany	4 087
3. France Telecom	France	2 449
4. BT	Britain	2 188
5. MCI	US	2 083
6. Swiss PTT	Switzerland	1 551
7. Stentor	Canada	1 520
8. Hong Kong Telecom	Hong Kong	1 137
9. Netherlands PTT	Netherlands	1 134
10. Itatel	Italy	1 116

[1]MITT = minutes of telecoms traffic

Source: *Financial Times* 15 November 1993

More importantly the corporate alliances outlined above will provide the fabric to bind together the key international markets: forming a EuroAmerican market. Over the rest of the 1990s competition will largely be played out in the market for services to multi-national companies. During this time, however, these large players will have the basis to gradually eat away at the monopolies of the former PTTs, especially outside the core countries of Germany, France and Britain. Into the next century what we can expect to see is a European,

Table 5.6　Global telecoms competition: progress compared

	1993		1997	
	% of exposed revenues	% held by competitors	% revenues	% held by competitors
Britain	100	10	100	22
Germany	7	0	30	3
France	7	0	30	4
Japan	50	7	50	15
USA	100	38	100	45

N.b. for Japan NTT used, USA AT&T used and Britain BT used

Source: Diawa Securities

if not global, market dominated by four or five major carriers.

The model of capitalism that takes hold of Europe in the next century will be partly shaped by events in the telecommunications industry. The privatisation of France Telecom is likely to follow the Eurocapitalism model, since the flotation will not be fully open to any subscribers. Indeed, it is likely that cross-shareholding between France Telecom and Deutshe Telekom is probable in this most crucial of future industries.

Although no two PTTs are the same, to complement this analysis of corporate trends within the telecommunications industry, it is useful to illuminate how the forces of liberalisation are driving change by a case study.

LIBERALISATION AND CORPORATE CHANGE IN SPANISH TELECOMMUNICATIONS: A CASE STUDY

The global trends outlined above are a major force in driving change in the individual member state telecommunications industries. Indeed, these global forces and corporate alliances have been significant in bringing about the implementation of liberalisation and privatisation of former state monopoly companies. A case study of the telecommunications industry in Spain illuminates these changes.

At the beginning of the 1900s there was a myriad of telephone service operators in Spain, most of which were local suppliers licensed by the state. The rapid development of a national and international telecommunications system led to the creation in 1924 of the single entity, Telefonica, to integrate all telephone services. In the aftermath of World War II the state took over the shareholding of ITT in Telefonica, ending with a minority 31 per cent control. The contract between Telefonica and the State signed in 1946 formed the basis for Telefonica's role in the telecommunications sector for the next 40 years. Indeed, little if anything changed during the period dominated by Franco's regime.

The 1986 accession of Spain to the European Union necessitated a modification of that framework and contractual relationship. Essentially the new agreement is an administrative organism subject to law. The earlier contract had a special legal status of its own. The new contract was bound to incorporate the newly established rules of the then European Community.

An important feature of the contract now in force is that it provides for deregulation of telecommunication services previously or currently under monopoly to Telefonica, except for the basic phone services available to all and the mobile phone services. Deregulation proper was to come about in 1993 (Table 5.7). Telefonica has held a critical position in this liberalisation process, not least because it dominates the market for services. Its share of the overall telecommunications market is around 55 per cent, comprising around 90 per cent of basic telephony services, and 95 per cent for basic public services including telex.

In recognising the potential threat to revenues made possible by the drafting of liberalisation rules in Brussels, Telefonica looked to its colonial relationships in South America. Telefonica now has holdings estimated at $5 billion in Latin America – the world's fastest growing economic region after the Far East. After being seen as being backward and running away from the European challenge, it is now seen as being visionary with global ambitions far beyond many of its parochial European counterparts. Telefonica started to invest in Latin America in the late 1980s, as Brussels formulated the

Table 5.7   Chronology of key liberalisation in Spanish telecommunications

	Liberalisation Date
Value-added Services	1987
Supplementary Telephones	1989
First Phone	1992
Radio Paging	1993
Data Transmission	1993
Private Mobile Phones	1994
2nd GSM Mobile Phone Operator	1994
Satellite Services	1994
Liberalisation of all Telephone Services	1998–2000

Source: Business Spain

liberalisation of the European market. The uncertain political situations kept many other telecoms companies at home. Since it first entered into this market in 1988, Telefonica now has interests in order of importance is Peru, Puerto Rico, Chile, Argentina, Venezuela and Uruguay. These footholds in a key market in the twenty-first century will be crucial in ensuring that Telefonica will be a major player, not just in Europe but in global markets.

SUMMARY

To sum up for this chapter, telecommunications provides perhaps the classic case of an industry that is being radically transformed by liberalisation. What the European telecommunications industry is witnessing is perhaps one of the most dramatic transitions ever seen in modern industrial economies from state to private control. But as this chapter has illustrated, this transition will not merely be a privatisation of state monopolies into private monopolies. What is emerging is a genuine liberalisation process in which Europe is seeing a range of new telecommunication carriers develop using an innovative variety of technologies to supply, not only voice, but data, text and vision transmission services. This process is extremely uneven in its pace and direction across the EU. However, there is an overall trend towards a multitude of suppliers in a rapidly fragmenting marketplace, that is at the core of the dynamics of industrial change as the millennium approaches.

The economic implications of the liberalisation of telecommunications across Europe, especially in terms of the number of job losses that the industry has seen, a problem that will continue to grow more severe. The impending deluge of redundancies that the industry must face can be gauged by what has happened in Britain since 1990 when employment peaked at 250 000. By 1993, this had fallen to 160 000, a fall of 90 000 or 36 per cent: many more have lost their jobs since. If this situation is replicated across the EU, then over a quarter of a million will be added to the dole queues. Indeed, by 1997 BT intends to have a workforce of just 100 000 so that six in every ten employees at the start of this decade will have lost their job with BT.

The ultimate dilemma for former European telecoms, especially those outside the big four of BT, France Telecom, the sleeping giant of Deutsche Telekom and the global reach of Telefonica, is to attract investment, at the same time as protecting revenues from new competition. The challenge for all European telecoms is to form, what the chairman of BT Sir Iain Vallence has termed, a complex hybrid – so that they can successfully sustain competitive threats from all sides. These competitive threats – as identified in this chapter – will have their genesis in three areas: the EuroAm market; universality and liberalisation, in particular open network provision; and the WMC revolution.

Notes

1. CEC (1993) *Growth, Competitiveness, Employment: The Challenges and Ways Forward into the 21st Century.* CEC. Brussels.
2. E. Noam (1992) *Telecommunications in Europe.* Longman. London, p. 305.
3. CEC (1987) *Communication 290.* CEC. Brussels.
4. CEC (1992) *The review of the situation in the telecommunications sector.* CEC 1048. Brussels.
5. CEC (1993) *Growth, Competitiveness, Employment: The Challenges and Ways Forward into the 21st Century.* CEC. Brussels, p. 1.
6. G. Edmondson (1994) Brave New World *Business Week* (Special Information Revolution Edition).
7. J. Cornford and A. Gillespie (1993) Cable systems, telephony and economic development in Britain *Telecommunications Policy* Vol. 14, 598–603.
8. See *The Economist* 16 July 1994.
9. McKinsey Management Consultancy (1992) *Service sector productivity.* McKinsey Global Institute. Washington DC, p. 2E.
10. McKinsey Management Consultancy (1992) *Service sector productivity.* McKinsey Global Institute. Washington DC.

6 After Liberalisation

INTRODUCTION

The rapid shifts that have resulted from liberalisation are transforming the very essence and structure of Europe's economy. The opening up of the world economy, with the almost universal adoption of the market philosophy, has radically altered the rules by which Europe must now compete. This change is not a one-off event. Nor is it one that will gradually diminish and lose momentum. It is a process that will gather pace and continue to radically refashion Europe for at least another a decade and a half; perhaps even two decades. A process that will fundamentally reshape Europe in the twenty-first century.

Liberalisation has unleashed significant forces of change that are powerfully combining with the information revolution to set in motion a new pattern of economic activity. This dynamic has set the world economy on a path of more integrated growth over the next 15 years. Indeed, the momentum carried forward by the current era of liberalisation is so strong that it is likely to maintain the world economy on its current path of economic development until 2010: without significant further liberalisation, regulation or protectionism at a global level. Two reasons underpin this projection.

First, around the world the ideology of the market will continue to sweep all before it. In the world's most dynamic economies, such as China, Singapore and Chile, the message of the market will be the powerful driving force that sustains high levels of growth. Central to this ideology is liberalisation of industrial, capital or labour markets. The second reason to explain the length of this period, is the fact that it will only be in the second decade of the next century that the disparities between developed and developing economies, such as wage levels, technology capabilities, and innovation capacity, will have diminished. It is only when this situation occurs that there will be the need, the will, and a degree of global economic equality to cause new institutions to be developed around the global economy.

It is important to note that this is not advocating the continued linear growth of the world economy. Rapid change, be it social or economic, carries with it the risk of political upheaval, war and poverty. Indeed, the speed of change which is rushing much of the world from an agrarian society towards the living standards of the west is bound to cause economic, political and social tensions. A microcosm of these tensions is most evident in early 1990s China. As China rushes headlong into capitalism, tensions are beginning to show created by the widely varying rates of economic development now taking place in the People's Republic. The flood of migrant workers from the rural interior to the special economic zones is placing huge tensions on the stability of Chinese society.

In the future, the death of Deng Xiaoping will have important consequences for the development of China as a unified nation. It is quite possible, with the death of Deng and the massive and growing disparities between the special economic zones on the eastern seaboard and the peasant dominated interior, that China will fracture and fragment or even erupt in civil war.

We have seen in this book how the global economic landscape has changed dramatically in recent years. The conclusion of the GATT talks has resulted in a new supra-national institution – the World Trade Organisation – which provides a framework to manage trade in goods and services over the next generation. In parallel with these developments has been the formation of regional trading blocs, which now dominate the global economy. There has been the unpredicted, but welcome fall of Communism; opening up vast areas of the world to the market economy. There has also been the unprecedented rise of developing economies – especially South East Asia and Latin America – that are taking the world economy by storm with their break-neck economic growth.

In this context, Europe now must meet the challenge of maintaining its prosperity in the face of a dynamic market economy. In the late 1980s and early 1990s, it has responded by building the world's largest single market and liberalising swathes of its align industry. This penultimate chapter evaluates the implications for Europe of this era of liberalisation. It assesses the balance between the imperative to remain a competitive global player in key industries – particularly high value-added services such as telecommunication services, computer services and financial services investigated in this book – and the side-effects for quality of life and the fabric of European society.

In doing so, this chapter analyses the future negative effects of liberalisation, for instance job losses resulting from the privatisation of state industries. This is contrasted with the much improved and continued need for better competitiveness of European industry, in the face of the new demands of the global economy. It adds to this equation the very mature demographic profile of Europe: a factor that will play a crucial role in its budgetary position over the next two decades.

EUROPE AFTER LIBERALISATION

This book has illustrated the seismic changes that are thundering through key service industries – the mainstay of the European economy in the twenty-first century. These individual changes have and will continue to reshape the economic landscape of Europe. The key thrust of this book, however, is that this is the cumulative effect of liberalisation, rather than just the impact on individual sectors, that is most important. Indeed, liberalisation has resulted in a quantum change in the composition of European industries, the structure of its markets, and above all a radical transformation of its economy.

There is little doubt that Europe was ill-prepared for the challenge posed by the rise of an integrated global economy. Much of the European economy was highly fragmented and based around national markets. As a consequence many industries were dominated by a handful of so-called national champions. The sectors investigated in this book illustrate this point. In financial services, a handful of banks in each of the EU 15 economies have dominated the market for retail financial services: Deutsche Bank, Commerzbank, and Dresdener Bank in Germany. In telecommunications, the national telephone companies have had a virtual monopoly of telecoms traffic in their country, be it Telecom Eireann in Ireland or Telefonica in Spain. While in computer services, companies such as Sema and Cap Gemini Sogeti dominated the French market. These national champions grew in the protected, monopolistic and regulated environs of post-war Europe.

Economies of scale and corporate might are now increasingly the determining factors of the new global economy. Within this context, it is plain that Europe had to liberalise to compete. It was this free-market logic that was behind the single European market programme and the current plans for economic and monetary union.

On the surface this policy has been successful, in that it has allowed major European corporations to leverage their domestic strengths as a platform to launch themselves into global competition. For example, in the telecommunications industry it has released BT, France Telecom and Deutsche Telekom to compete in the emerging global market to provide seamless, one-stop international services to trans-national corporations (TNCs). For smaller telecoms companies, it has offered the opportunity to band together to form alliances that can compete in this new marketplace. For instance, take the international link up between the Swedish, Swiss and Dutch national telecommunication companies, under the Unisource banner.

The liberalisation of the European economy was also required to enable the better allocation of resources. The single market, as we have already noted, was a patchwork of markets and national champions. In the context of the global economy, this is not an effective combination to compete against the might of the NAFTA and ASEAN trade blocs, nor giant US and Japanese TNCs. These measures have allowed Europe to move along the path of reducing domestic economic costs. Of course central to achieving this aim will be full economic and monetary union; a single currency will radically reduce costs within Europe.

In addition, creating and increasing economies of scale both within the European economy and individual firms was achieved by breaking national monopolies, cartels and restrictive practices. An important key in opening up national markets has been to expose, often sizeable, state industries to the rigours of the market. As discussed in Chapter 2, it has been necessary for Europe to run privatisation hand-in-hand with liberalisation. This process has seen a historic shift in the ownership of business from state to private ownership – an unprecedented shake-up. Since Britain began its sell-off of its national telephone company, BT in 1983, a deluge of privatisation has swept across Europe valued at $100 billion[1].

Flowing from these privatisations has been the advantage that they have relieved pressure on government budgets. Indeed, privatisation has generated significant revenues for state coffers. This is, however, only a short-term gain. The long-term benefit of liberalisation will be the reductions in public spending from the absence of no longer supporting non-commercial state industries. The pressure of government debt will be a major challenge facing European governments in the next century. The spread of the market philosophy has also had the effect of reducing state subsidies; in particular a reduction in the CAP (Common Agricultural Policy). To quote Alexis Jacquemin and David Wright[2], 'Europe will never be economically efficient subsiding milk and sugar, rather than biotechnology and electronics'.

For the consumer, the benefits of liberalisation have been particularly attractive. The injection of competition into cartels and the dismantling of regulation has resulted in improved choice and service quality. The privatisation of state public services has brought these companies into direct competition with the private sector – often across European borders. Take the example of airlines, where the transfer of national carriers from state to private ownership has resulted in cheaper flights and better services.

In the future, a major benefit will accrue to Europe from the liberalisation of its infrastructure network. This is taking place through the removal of the barriers to all types of communications infrastructure from railways to energy, roads to telecommunications. By opening up competition on these routeways it is hoped to attract private sector capital investment, so at to achieve the dual aim of reducing government spending and increasing the modernisation of these networks.

The parting shot of Jacques Delors from his long reign at the European Commission (EC) was his White Paper[3] on opening up Europe's infrastructure arteries, so as to improve EU interconnectivity and business competitiveness. The aim of the Delors decree was that liberalisation can play a part in extending these networks beyond national boundaries by drawing in private capital; knitting together Europe's diverse and fragmented markets. The completion and operation of the Channel Tunnel is a successful case in point.

The information economy of the twenty-first century will be a key growth area – again liberalisation has enhanced Europe's position. The liberalisation of telecommunications networks is particularly vital to the future competitiveness of regions, companies and individuals[4]. In telecommunications, the EC has promoted the notion of open network provision (ONP) as the basis for improved competitiveness through an open digital infrastructure. However, to a great extent these events are being overtaken by the mushrooming growth of the Internet. The powerful forces of new information networks are proving too strong for bureaucrats in Brussels – reflecting the might of the shaping forces of globalisation.

Finally, the liberalisation of service industries is particularly significant for the future prosperity of Europe. There are two reasons for this. First, service industries will be at the vanguard of developments in the world economy over the next decade: generating new employment, but also in designing, marketing and servicing manufactured goods. Second, the next decade is likely to see the largest ever gains in the liberalisation of services at a global level. A central part of the remit for the WTO is to carry forward the momentum of GATT in bringing about the managed liberalisation of services. For instance, financial services were not included in the final GATT deal. In a world context, liberalisation has been driven by the increasing tradability of services. The key determinant in allowing the growth in tradable services is a sophisticated and liberalised telecommunications infrastructure. Taken together, these developments should leave Europe well placed for growth in the next century.

Overall, as a result of liberalisation the competitiveness of European business has improved. With an eye on the future, it was particularly important that Europe opened up its service industries to compete in the knowledge economy of the twenty-first century. It was also essential that it dismantled the barriers that fragmented its indigenous economies. Liberalisation has also been important in allowing the market to perform a better allocation of resources. Liberalisation together with privatisation has yielded for the consumer significant benefits in terms of better service and lower prices. Europe has undoubtedly benefited from liberalisation.

BEYOND LIBERALISATION

There are some essential caveats to add to this analysis, however. It is important to recognise that although Europe continues to harness and exploit the economies of scale of a single market, it will remain for at least another decade a patchwork of cultures, tastes and economic practices – this in spite of the homogenising effects of liberalisation. Free markets are not a panacea for unifying Europe, nor should they be.

There are three key factors that will continue to mediate the forces of liberalisation – meaning that even in the next century Europe will largely retain its diversity.

First, there is the rather straightforward point that all European countries are different. As explained in Chapter 2, Europe's economies in the post-war period were based around stringent national regulation. This involved taking a significant number of industries into public ownership. The level of public ownership and degree of regulation was very distinct to each country. As a result, when responding to the directives issued by the European Commission to liberalise industries under the 1992 banner each country has interpreted these in different ways. From Chapter 5, take the example of Deutsche Telekom, which has to overcome the fact that all its employees are civil servants and therefore entitled to a job for life. This example illustrates that each European country is very different in the implementation of the liberalising decrees.

Second, liberalisation will continue to affect countries in different ways, because of the different business cultures that exist in the 15 countries in the EU. Most significant in translating the impacts of liberalisation is the type of corporate governance: that is the legal framework, institutional rules and ownership criteria that businesses must operate within that country. These are different in every European economy. For example, corporate taxation levels are different in every country, hence a TNC has to have a legal subsidiary in every country that it operates in, rather than a single European company.

Also, systems of corporate governance differ according to the regulations and arrangements governing the dispersion and diffusion of corporate ownership and the methods of monitoring management performance. These, in turn, affect patterns of corporate financing and industrial structure. Corporate governance, therefore, has a significant bearing over how liberalisation affects the relative performance of an economy.

The third factor that mediates the impact of liberalisation is the industrial structure of an economy. Again across Europe there are varying degrees of industrial concentration – that is the proportion of a market that is supplied by each firm in that market. The number of trans-national corporations operating in an economy is often determined by the openness of that economy to the international marketplace. It often reflects to some extent an inherent weakness of that economy. The industrial structure of the domestic economy is important too. Germany, for example, is famous for its Mittlestand (small and medium size companies) that are credited with the platform for the post-war success of Germany. The industrial structure is also influenced by the level of state control and the degree of privatised industries.

The example of Italy illustrates how the impact of liberalisation is mediated and translated by these factors. The Italian economy is characterised by a small number of large business conglomerates. These include Italian industrial giants such as Fiat, Ferruzzi, Olivetti, Generali and Pirelli; companies such as these employing more than 2 000 staff account for over 16 per cent of the workforce. The closeness of this community is reflected by the fact that a single bank – Mediobank – has some degree of controlling interest in every one of these large concerns. By contrast, these large conglomerates coexist alongside a vast network of small and medium companies. Italy has the highest proportion of such firms compared with Germany, France, USA and Japan. Often these types of firms are found within so-called industrial districts – dense networks of family-owned companies specialising in the production of high quality goods. In Italy, liberalising directives from Brussels have not penetrated very deeply into the network of small firms or large conglomerates, or significantly broken these ownership structures, because of Italy's unique business structures. The influence of liberalisation is and will continue to be moderated by such corporate governance structures.

However, of far greater importance is the impact of liberalisation on European society. The benefits that have flowed from the opening up of markets have been essential and significant in maintaining a rising standard of living that many Europeans have become accustomed to. Nonetheless, substantial further liberalisation may seriously threaten the very basis of European society. This is the challenge that awaits Europe's leaders and policy-makers in the twenty-first century.

EXCESSIVE LIBERALISATION THREATENS THE FUTURE PROSPERITY OF EUROPE

Liberalisation has engendered Europe with a greater degree of competitiveness in the global economy. However, this has been achieved at a great cost. It is possible to gauge the cost of liberalisation through the following: the rise in unemployment; the loss of corporate control; the end of universality of service; and the widening gap between rich and poor. Cumulatively this is leading to incredible strains and tensions within European society. Can social cohesion withstand further pressures of market liberalisation, if Europe is to remain competitive in the world economy of the twenty-first century?

First, the most pressing problem facing Europe is the seemingly unstoppable upward rise in unemployment. The opening up of the European economy to the competitive forces of change in the international economy has coincided with the increase in the jobless total. Most significant over the last decade has been the fact that although economic growth has moved through its traditional economic cycles, unemployment has continued on an upward trend. This phenomenon, known as jobless growth, can be laid squarely at the door of liberalisation.

Over the last 20 years unemployment has increased in the EU 12 from a low of around 3 per cent in 1971, to a high of 11 per cent in 1994 – it also peaked at this level in the mid-1980s[5]. The significance of opening up economies to international competition is demonstrated by what has happened in former European Free Trade Association (EFTA) countries. Over the last five years the liberalising reforms have pushed unemployment sky-high. For instance, the average jobless total in EFTA was just over 2 per cent in 1989, but this has climbed steeply to 8 per cent by 1993. Finland has suffered the most, there the rate rose from 3 per cent to 18 per cent between 1991 and 1993.

In the face of these trends, it must also be recognised that Europe will not be able to compete in the zero sum productivity game of the future. It is already plain that the emerging economies of the developing world can outpace levels of productivity and unit labour costs achieved in Europe. Competitiveness in the next century will be based around quality goods, with excellence in design and development, rather than just cost. By continuing with such a high level of structural unemployment, Europe is in effect storing up problems for the twenty-first century. Since a growing minority of the workforce will be unable to have the opportunity to constantly up-date their work experience, this will create a significant and highly problematic skills gap. Governments will either have to spend billions on re-training schemes, or leave this portion of society to survive on low-wage, low-skill service employment: the so-called McJobs. The cost of such a solution to social cohesion will indeed be significant.

The second negative impact of liberalisation has been the significant loss of corporate control. The freeing up of Europe's economies has opened wide the opportunity for national champions to be acquired by global corporations or competing national champions from elsewhere in the single market. Evidence from the computer services industry illustrates how Europe, and Britain in particular, over the last decade has lost many of its leading firms in this sector to US companies.

It is hotly debated whether the ownership of firms and industries is important in running a successful economy. It is argued that the loss of corporate control leads to the removal of key strategy and investment decisions to the head-office of the controlling corporation – stifling innovation, for instance. To counter this point, it must be noted that TNCs are becoming increasingly disloyal to any national ties. Hence, the notion of a borderless corporation with no country loyalty will become a feature of the next century.

However, loss of corporate control has had a negative impact largely because of the national orientation of companies in Europe. Loss of ownership leads to a break-up of patterns of procurement and suppliers that surrounded these national champions in the past. These changes have contributed to the rise in the jobless total around Europe. This trend will continue. For instance, in the car market it is unlikely that six high-volume producers with around 15 per cent of the market will survive, especially as the restrictions on Japanese manufacturers are removed. Higher industrial concentration, which has eliminated many smaller players, will go further in the first decade of the next century.

Another major negative effect of liberalisation on European society has been the loss of universality of service provision. During the post-war era, the establishment of state utilities was based around the notion that each citizen was granted equal geographical access to essential services. These varied by country, but ranged from health services to telephony services, to energy and banking services. Liberalisation has destroyed the universality of service provision, since it has made transparent the cross-subsidisation within the organisations that provided such services. Allied to this trend has been the liberalisation of public procurement contracts under EU law.

After liberalisation, those peripheral areas or portions of society that are at the margin find it harder to access the same level of service – if at all. This is because one of the key outcomes of liberalisation is that it removes cross-subsidisation; both geographically and socially. Universality of provision has been protected by regulation in the majority of countries. The privatisation of former state industries is reducing access to services for some of the less wealthy sections of society. In particular, the transfer of utilities from state to private ownership has removed the requirement for cross-subsidisation. Therefore, in rural districts without heavy population density it is more difficult to get access to a service and it is likely to cost more, a cost that was hidden when the service was provided by the state. Within a society that is seeing a growing gulf between rich and poor, will ending access to such essential services further increase these social tensions?

The need for a correct balance is illustrated by attempts in the USA to design telecoms regulation that allows the notion of universality to live side-by-side the market.

Finally, the quality of life in Europe is widely regarded as one of the best in the world. The high level of public services, the quality of the environment and the relatively low level of crime are envied all over the globe. The net effect of liberalisation is adding millions to the dole queues of Europe, placing this situation under pressure. The resulting and widening gap between rich and poor adds a new dimension to European society, not seen since the 1930s depression.

The cutting of red tape and intense competition from developing economies has pushed some industries to reduce the cost of treating waste from industrial processes. The growing level of acid rain bears witness to this trend. This is in spite of the rapid growth in EC environmental directives. The rising level of unemployment is also leading to higher levels of crime on Europe's once peaceful and sedate streets. Although still nothing like the USA this is a worrying trend. Indeed, these trends are combining together to make the social fabric, that gives Europe such a high quality of life, increasingly threadbare.

It is not just a negative social impact that liberalisation has imparted on Europe. The pressure that liberalisation has placed on these social structures has implications for small firm networks: the lifeblood of many European countries. The social market economies of Germany and Italy provided the environment that nurtured the successful small firm networks that have provided the platform for employment, economic growth and prosperity. The impact of further liberalisation could fracture and fragment these networks. This would be paramount to economic suicide for many European economies.

The twenty-first century will also have a greyer tint to it than the past few decades – two-thirds of those over 65 who have ever lived in Europe are alive today. The baby booms that hit Europe after the end of World War II and the hedonistic sixties will mean that Europe will have a maturing demographic profile in the early decades of the next century. This will place new pressure on welfare systems, in addition to coping with the fallout of the widening divide between the haves and have-nots.

The cost is already placing stress on the public finances and international competitiveness of much of Europe.

Undoubtedly the ageing demographic structure of Europe will alter patterns of consumption, production, employment, savings, investment and innovation. More specifically, the burden of pensions could double over the next 50 years, through a combination of an ageing population and the increased cost of covering pensions. At the same time, the ratio of working Europeans to pensioners will continue to fall until around 2030. The problem is most acute in Europe's power-house Germany, where there will be only three working people to every over-65 person by 2010. By contrast, developing economies will gain a further competitive advantage through from their much younger populations.

In sum, further excessive liberalisation of Europe's economy will fundamentally inhibit its ability to compete in the global economy of the twenty-first century. The recovery of Europe's major economies in the post-war decades, perhaps with the exception of Britain, has been quite remarkable. The increase in living standards and wealth has been within a framework of high welfare provision. The liberalisation of these institutions and structures will remove the cornerstone around which this success has been built. This is not to deny that Europe needs to modernise its economic cultures, practices and structures. There is still a significant need for improvement. The pension systems of most European states are ill prepared to cope with the approaching demographic time-bomb. Nonetheless, the social fabric of Europe will tear under the pressure of further liberalisation – a message that must be heeded in Brussels in future policy-making. Rather than further slashing of regulations, Europe must look to new ways of gaining global competitiveness in the next century. In order to do this we must understand the shape of the world in the dawn of a new century.

Notes

1. Morgan Stanley (1994) *European Privatisations*. Morgan Stanley.
2. A. Jacquemin and D. Wright (1993) *European Challenges Post 1992*. Elgar, p. 94.
3. CEC (1993) White Paper. *Growth, Competitiveness, Employment*. CEC. Brussels.
4. N. Negroponte (1995) *Being Digital*. Hodder and Stoughton. London.
5. EC (1994) *Employment in Europe*.

7 Europe in 2010

It is not possible to forecast the exact shape and outcome of any economic process – especially over a 15-year period. For the world becomes ever more complex, as the multitude of forces that can potentially combine together become ever more great and diverse. However, what it is possible is to sketch the broad trends. Events taking place today are set on a trend that will not drastically change over the coming decade, especially if the short-term platform that we use to project trends has become firmly established. The weight of change behind these forces means that they have momentum that will carry them forward.

As has been stressed throughout this book, it is developments in the global economy that will set the context in which Europe will develop. What will the world economy in 2010 look like?

The first major trend to note over the next two decades will be the continued growth of developing economies. The last five years have seen the emergence of dramatic changes in the global economy, most notably the integration of the developed and the developing world. This has been a significant change, from the major debts developing countries built up in the 1970s and 1980s, to the early 1990s where major flows of investment capital are pouring into these nations. This is just the start of the emergence of these economies. Liberalising reforms will mean that by 2010 countries such as Chile, Argentina and Brazil in South America, and Malaysia, Indonesia and Thailand in South East Asia will have attained full industrialisation. There will, however, be casualties along the road. In early 1995, for instance, the collapse of the Mexican economy was so severe that it set its economic reforms back many years. It also highlighted the need for economic change to go hand-in-hand with democratic change. The corrupt PRI – the political party – that has held unbroken power for over 50 years in Mexico still poses it major problems.

Thus far, excluded from this analysis has been any mention of China. It is unquestionable that over the next 15 years China will rise to be one of the leading industrial nations in the world economy. This will not be a smooth passage. The end of the Deng Xiaoping era will lead to much turmoil – possibly civil war in China.

China's emergence on to the world stage will also be marked by unrest. For it is unlikely that China will easily slot into the institutional structures in which the global economy is framed. Within the new global trading environment of the World Trade Organisation, tension has already been created by attempting to get China elected. Once China is a full and active member of such global institutions, it will continue to flex its muscles. The key consequence of this is likely to be a new global economic 'cold war' between China and the USA. The trade wars of the early 1990s between USA and Japan will be even more bitterly replayed in the early years of the next century with China.

Another key feature of the global economy of the early twenty-first century will be the increasing dominance of transnational corporations (TNCs). As Chapter 2 demonstrated, TNCs will continue to gain greater sway in the free markets of the 1990s and 2000s. The borderless corporation will be a common feature. Increasingly geographically mobile, and with diminishing home country loyalty, the TNCs of the twenty-first century will, more and more, rival the sovereign power of countries.

TNCs will also drive change within economies. They will achieve this in part through the shift in the changing locus of power in buyer–supplier relationships towards corporations. This will be a consequence of both new technologies and the growing importance of economies of scale. The power of the media industry in conveying the message of the multinational also should not be underestimated in bringing about the growing domination of global markets by a handful of corporations. This is not to deny that small firms will still be critical to the vitality of local economies, both as a source of employment and a generator of wealth.

Another key driver of the future world economy will be the further shift to the information economy. The rapid developments that the digital revolution has brought to economic activity in the early 1990s have been almost revolutionary in their impact. The technological possibilities are even greater over the next 15 years. Once the world has a digital communications infrastructure in place – which will happen within the next decade – then the information revolution will take its full course. A parallel development, with the growth of these networks, will be the gradual homogenisation of knowledge around the world. This will gradually erode the competitive advantage of developed economies. These changes will culminate together to have a significant impact between 2005 and 2010. By then a spatial division of labour between service industries will have taken place to match the migration from manufacturing in the 1980s and 1990s.

By 2010, it will be necessary for the global economy to reform its institutional structures to match a world economy that will look very different. However, change will not happen all at once. In the short term, there is a growing need for supranational laws to sit alongside the WTO. The rapid growth in foreign direct investment has created a whole new industry dedicated to attracting capital into economies, regions and cities. Many resources are wasted by organisations and governments attempting to bring this investment to their (most depressed) regions – increasingly even prosperous cities have their own inward investment agencies such as Barcelona, London and Paris. TNCs are also taking advantage of this system playing one area off against another to achieve the maximum subsidy for their investment – which could doubtless be made anywhere. This is a zero-sum game. International rules would go some way towards creating a more level playing field to reduce FDI competition.

The second area where there is a need for concerted action on a global level is labour conditions. The United Nations needs to build a treaty to sit alongside GATT/WTO rules on labour conditions. The growing evidence is that part of the developing world's wealth is based on the exploitation of child labour, which needs to be stopped. Surely, a decent place – and only at 16 years of age – to work is a basic human right.

To summarise, the world economy in 2010 will have developed into something quite different from that in the 1990s. The gap between the developed and the developing world will have significantly diminished. Many of the countries that are today newly industrialising will have attained full industrialisation. Beneath the surface, however, there will still be considerable disparities between rich and poor. Africa, for instance, will still be extremely poor, since it has none of the ingredients – education, skills, digital communications infrastructure – that are required for success in the twenty-first century. Also within these maturing industrialised countries the disparities between an expanding professional middle class and unemployed working class will grow ever greater. Russia will continue to be plagued by domestic problems. In spite of the growing wealth, these differences will on a world scale cause social, resource and environmental tensions, that mean that civil war and strife will not disappear in this new world order. Overall, the world should have fewer wars, less poverty and greater prosperity.

EUROPE IN 2010

In the wake of these forces what will Europe look like in 2010? Two aspects of the European economy will be particularly important in determining its future over the next 15 years. First, to what extent can it generate economies of scale to improve global competitiveness? The most decisive factor here will be the adoption of a single currency. Will Europe have a single currency by 2010? And if it does: which countries will participate? What benefits will they derive?

Second, how will Europe be able to differentiate itself in the new global marketplace? How important will flexibility to market change be? Will the regions of Europe be able to produce high value, quality goods and services to export to a growing world market? All this will be dependent on the shape and structure of Europe in 2010. How will Europe look in 2010?

In spite of remaining as a diverse set of economies, Europe will have moulded itself into a unified single market, with significant economies of scale. The creation of a single market in the early 1990s will be seen retrospectively as a successful and necessary action for Europe to maintain a leading role in the world.

The world economy of the twenty-first century will demand even greater economies of scale to compete. Europe will have attained a greater level of industrial might. Liberalisation will have freed many of Europe's national champions from the shackles of their national markets, allowing international expansion.

However, the most significant event to generate greater industrial power for Europe over the next decade and a half will be the adoption of a single currency. By 2010, the Euro will have been adopted by each of the current EU 15 – a common currency for all. It will not be a smooth transition, however. The benefits that will accrue to the EU by adopting a single currency fall into three broad areas. First, there will be a need for those countries that enter EMU to adopt sound monetary and fiscal polices in the transition to a currency union. This will enable these economies to gain more credibility in the money markets, resulting in a more stable interest rate environment. The second set of benefits that will flow from the adoption of a single currency are the elimination of intra-European transaction costs. The eradication of these distortions will have a direct impact by reducing costs throughout Europe. Thirdly, efficiency gains from the ending of currency transaction costs will be significant. The abolition of such practices will also generate efficiencies in accounting and monitoring procedures such as compilation of national accounts.

The adoption of a single money for Europe will not take place all at once, rather it will happen in three stages – with groups of countries joining at various stages during the next 15 years. The basis for this view is the current and future synchronisation of business cycles in the EU. It is this relationship between economies that will determine the feasibility of each joining a unified currency system. In part, it is also due to the way the era of liberalisation has been adopted and mediated by the different economies.

The core countries of Europe, which have seen greatest stability as their economies have become more closely tied together, will continue to be closely synchronised. This group includes the Netherlands, Belgium and Luxembourg, Austria and, of course, Germany. It is possible that these countries will have attained a common currency by the turn of the century. The sentimental impetus that surrounds achieving a single currency by the millennium should not be underestimated. France may also be part of this group. It will strive hard to anchor itself to Germany, to ensure that its Teutonic rival does not gain any advantage. Long-term economic fundamentals are against France, however.

The current synchronisation of business cycles suggests that France will potentially lead the second round of countries to join a European single currency in 2002. It will be joined by Switzerland – which by this time will have reconsidered its referendum and decided that the magnetism of the EU is irresistible – along with Denmark, Spain, Italy and Ireland. These countries will join largely because of political will to remain at the heart of Europe, rather than a close economic correlation with the core countries. It is essential that France, Spain and Italy do join a currency union at this time, since it will require political commitment, along with economic fundamentals. It is also possible that Britain will adopt a single currency at this stage too. The key factor here is whether the British Labour Party win the next election. If they do, then it is quite possible that Britain's appetite for becoming more heavily involved in a united Europe will grow.

By 2005, all the remaining countries will have joined the single currency union. In this group will be the Scandinavian economies of Sweden and Finland. It is possible that Norway will also reverse its decision not to join the EU, and attain membership and adopt the Euro rapidly. Finally, there will be Portugal and Greece. It is likely that Portugal could be part of a currency union by 2005. However, in the case of Greece economic fundamentals point to great difficulties in attaining suitable conditions to be adopted into the new monetary system of Europe. The criteria will remain strict. The European Central Bank – based in Frankfurt – will be run under tight guidelines, which will be heavily influenced by its German host.

Overall, the European economy in 2010 will be very different from that in the mid-1990s. The most striking difference will be in the provision of goods and services. The European market will be dominated by a range of pan-European providers, be it in financial services, retailing, telecommunications or food processing. To the consumer in Palermo or Stockholm, it might be branded or packaged in a different way to meet the needs and tastes of very diverse cultures. But corporate ownership will be heavily concentrated amongst a handful of powerful providers. However, Europe will very much remain a patchwork of tastes and cultures.

Europe will be dominated by an even closer Franco–German relationship. This alliance will be stronger due to cross-ownership of corporations, infrastructural links and nearly a decade of a single currency. For instance, it is likely that Germany and France will use their financial and economic systems to bond together privatised and liberalised companies, so that neither loses an influence over strategic industries. At the heart of such developments will be the telecommunication giants, Deutsche Telekom and France Telecom, and even the rail networks DBB and SNCF. Germany – together with its Benelux partners – will be very much the leading partner in this match, as France struggles to provide a counter to the increasing eastward dominance of its neighbour, and thus retain an influence over the direction that Europe follows.

As for the other leading nations, Italy and Spain will become more tightly tied together. In liberalising their economies these two nations will look to a common bond to exert influence in the EU. Italy will lag behind France in its economic performance – mainly because of its problem with public finances: France will shun Italy to concentrate on its relationship with Germany. Hence, Italy will be looking for a partner of roughly equal importance and economic credentials. Britain will not suffice, the countries have little in common in terms of their overall aims for Europe. Italy, therefore, will look for a pro-Europe economy that is gaining in influence. Spain will have similar interests. The two countries will also have experienced similar problems introducing market reforms, and transferring state industries over to the market. Liberalisation will reinforce the significant regional problems that these two countries face. Also, it is likely that by 2010 both these countries will have introduced further federalisation, with more autonomy being granted to increasingly restless regions. This will provide another spur for these two nations to find strength in mutual support. Spain, as it continues its rapid industrialisation, will leave the so-called 'Cohesion Four' group – Ireland, Portugal and Greece – and gain importance and influence within the EU.

Britain and Ireland will continue their close relationship. However, Ireland will increasingly look for (economic) independence through closer ties with the EU – it will achieve this by 2010 with a united Ireland. For Britain, a future in

Europe will become more certain when and if the Labour Party wins control from the anti-federalist Conservative Party. Britain has led much of Europe in improving economic efficiency – due to the whole-hearted fashion with which it has embraced the market. However, this will come at a cost. The effects of market reform will bring a heavy social cost in terms of unemployment and a sizeable underclass. These will impede Britain's growth in the next century. However, it will look increasingly eastwards, both politically and economically, reducing its ties with the USA.

With large variations in growth rates, the Cohesion Four will disband. The futures of Spain and Ireland have already been discussed. Different fates await Portugal and Greece. For Portugal the horizon is bright. It will continue to pursue a rigorous monetary policy that will win it many friends in the EU. It will remain near the bottom of Europe's prosperity league, but overall living standards will rise significantly. Market reforms will mean that the country attracts much foreign capital. In the process it will lose control of much of its industry. By contrast, Greece faces a Herculean task to 'catch up' with its European partners. It is likely that it will not be able to make significant progress in this direction. While it will remain in the EU, it is possible that over the next decade it will become increasingly involved in the fiery local politics of the Balkans. Further tensions will be caused by Turkey – its bitter rival – attempting to join the EU.

The Scandinavian countries will slowly become more integrated into the EU. By 2010, Norway – along with Switzerland – will be members of the EU. These economies will experience some problems building a bond with the rest of the EU. Not least it will require new infrastructure routes to tie the two areas closer together. Market reforms are likely to be painful, as will be the relative fall in the standard of living that will accompany these changes. However, by the end of the first decade of the next century, Sweden, Norway and Finland will be fully integrated into the EU.

Finally, there will be an eastwards expansion of the EU. By 2010, countries such as the Czech Republic, Hungary and Poland will have received associate membership of the EU. Central Europe will be an important economic resource to the EU. First, it will provide a low-cost, accessible location in which to manufacture. It will also provide a large market for the export of EU goods, especially capital goods as these countries move along the path of industrialisation. How will all these changes leave Europe positioned in the world economy of 2010? And, what will be the factors that will make it successful in the twenty-first century? What must Europe do to maintain social cohesion, while at the same time improving global competitiveness?

LIBERALISATION WHERE POSSIBLE, REGULATION WHERE NECESSARY

Europe must soon decide that to achieve global competitiveness with social cohesion intact, the economies that have banded together to form the EU cannot sustain another round of liberalisation of a similar intensity as has occurred over the last decade. For the introduction of another round of market forces would leave in shreds the fabric that holds Europe together.

Clearly, the ever increasing speed of developments in the global economy means that Europe must continuously modernise its economy. This alone will not be enough, however. To gain a competitive advantage it is essential that Europe plans for the future. It must identify those features of its economy that will give it an advantage in the global economy of the twenty-first century, but will also benefit its people. It is exactly this balance that Europe can achieve in the future – using the maxim: liberalisation where possible, regulation where necessary.

The shift from closed monopolistic markets to free markets brings with it the need to develop regulatory mechanisms to monitor the liberalised markets. Britain is at the forefront of developments, in particular in the area of utilities. Here it has built a comprehensive set of regulators, which have powers to reduce prices and act in the interests of the consumer. There are lessons to be learnt for the rest of Europe, the British system is too heavily orientated towards the individual who runs each of the regulators. The challenge for Europe then is: how to build a regulatory system that harnesses the benefits of market liberalisation, but also protects the consumer. This can only be achieved by implementing liberalisation where possible, regulation where necessary. This is important since the regulator – the European Commission – can play a key role in maintaining better social cohesion, by moderating the worst aspects of the free market.

How might Europe build a better competitive advantage? There are six key issues that Europe must develop, if it is to build a genuine global competitive advantage by 2010. The issues are: employment; training; science; corporate architecture; single market; and global perspectives.

Liberalisation has and will continue to add thousands to Europe's jobless total. It has given rise to significant structural unemployment. Policies must be developed that address this problem, rather than waiting for the total to be eroded by economic upturns. Europe needs to solve its problem of jobless growth. It needs to create employment intensive growth. There are a range of possible solutions. Lowering the burdens on employers, thus reducing non-wage costs. New types of work. Combinations of part-time work, job-share schemes or reducing the working week. The answer will not be in cutting wages – Europe cannot compete in the global marketplace in this way.

Training must come as standard, if Europe is to have a workforce to compete in the twenty-first century. Tomorrow's markets will demand products and services that are state-of-the-art, high quality and low price. To achieve this Europe must constantly invest in its human resources. Companies need to undergo a cultural shift to recognise that personal skills development will add value to their products and services. Training will gather increasing importance as the shift to the information economy picks up speed in the next century.

Science will play a critical role in Europe's future over the next 15 years. As competition intensifies, more and more pressure will be placed on the ability to be innovative: a company must have access to the latest thinking on research and development. Access to this information allows rapid new product development. This alone is not enough. Europe needs to get better at the two D's: design and development. For taking a prototype from the laboratory to the marketplace is not easy. However, by building skills in design and development Europe will have the capability to exploit commercial opportunities from generic ideas. Companies must think about these opportunities in a global context. Too often in the past Europe has been considered the only market; the global market has not been targeted.

A key barometer to the performance of Europe in the twenty-first century will be the number of global companies that have their origins in Europe. European companies cannot compete by cutting costs. This will not be enough. What is required is a systematic redesign of the company, to embrace new practices that will engender companies with a real competitive advantage. Central to this will be the adoption of process redesign so as to enhance the quality of goods and services. Companies need to empower their workforce. For instance, wider share-ownership amongst a company's employees needs to be encouraged. Companies also need to build teams and loyalty, as well as flexibility and strategic vision – if they are to be successful by 2010.

In the next century, the single market must give Europe the economies of scale to compete at a global level. This means that the current process of liberalising national markets must be rapidly implemented. Europe must exploit the size of the market, and at the same time maintain its specialisms in particular industries. In many ways Europe has stolen a march on the other trade blocs. Its process of liberalisation – although often criticised as bureaucratic – is a role model of how to bring about an integration of numerous countries into a unified economy. This is a real advantage. One which may even be adopted at a global level – after 2010.

Finally, Europeans must increasingly think with global vision. The world has shrunk, both in communications times and travelling times. It will continue to do so. It is therefore imperative that individuals, companies and governments think about the interconnections within the global economy. What new opportunities do these changes have? What threats do they pose to Europe? Events are taking place at an ever increasing speed. If Europe does not adopt a global vision in the twenty-first century, it will be at a significant competitive disadvantage.

These factors must be added to Europe's greatest asset: its diversity. The diversity of Europe is its Achilles' heel; however, it is also its most valuable future asset. The challenge of the next century is not about how to achieve economies of scale:

that was very much a twentieth century problem. The future of business competitiveness will lie in the ability to combine economies of scale together with local tastes and service: this is true for firms and economies alike. Indeed, it is a mistake to view the diversity of the European economy as a disadvantage or a handicap on the region's global competitiveness. The direction of economic activity over the coming decade will mean that those economies, which can be flexible, produce high quality goods and export to the international economy, will be successful.

Europe matches this trend in two ways. First, because many of Europe's individual markets do not have the domestic demand to sustain companies, they must look to new markets. Europe's companies are adept at learning to translate new market opportunities and to adapt a product to fit a market need. This ability must now be applied to the global market.

Second, many of Europe's successes have been built on intensive specialisation. For instance, German capital goods, British pharmaceuticals and Italian luxury goods. Companies are continuously striving to create and enhance distinctive competitive advantages. Often these have grown out of the local marketplace. Europe must now combine economies of scale from the single market with diverse and differentiated goods and services.

Liberalisation has irrevocably changed Europe's economy for the better. At the same time, further liberalisation will tear the fabric of European society through excessive unemployment, which could damage the very platform on which Europe has built its post-war prosperity. In chasing the Asian Tigers, Europe could undermine the prosperity and diversity that will provide it with the basis for a competitive advantage in the global economy in an era after liberalisation. Europe has that competitive advantage in the diversity of its industries and quality of its goods and services. Europe must rise to this challenge.

Index